Representation

Representation

Mónica Brito Vieira
David Runciman

polity

First published in 2008 by Polity Press

Polity Press
65 Bridge Street
Cambridge CB2 1UR, UK

Polity Press
350 Main Street
Malden, MA 02148, USA

ISBN-13: 978-07456-4159-1
ISBN-13: 978-07456-4160-7 (pb)

A catalogue record for this book is available from the British Library.

Typeset in 10.5 on 12 pt Sabon
by SNP Best-set Typesetter Ltd., Hong Kong
Printed and bound in Great Britain by MPG Books Ltd, Bodmin, Cornwall

The publisher has used its best endeavours to ensure that the URLs for external websites referred to in this book are correct and active at the time of going to press. However, the publisher has no responsibility for the websites and can make no guarantee that a site will remain live or that the content is or will remain appropriate.

Every effort has been made to trace all copyright holders, but if any have been inadvertently overlooked the publishers will be pleased to include any necessary credits in any subsequent reprint or edition.

For further information on Polity, visit our website: www.polity.co.uk

Contents

Figures and Tables

Figures

Tables

Preface

When it comes to representation, one thing, but perhaps only one thing, is undeniable: it is a concept that encompasses an extraordinary range of meanings and applications, stretching from mental images to economic transactions, and from legal process to theatrical performance. These various yet related senses of the term are all implicated, if not confused, in ongoing debates about political representation. Our aim in this book is to bring out the many different strands that are contained in the concept of representation, without losing sight of its absolute centrality for modern politics. Accounts of representation often pursue one or other of these goals, but not usually both. When the concept of representation is explored in its various different guises – particularly when the discussion moves towards representation considered as an aesthetic, legal or philosophical idea – then the focus tends to drift away from politics. Meanwhile, specifically political treatments of representation are liable to impose an artificial uniformity on the concept, pinning it down to a particular definition or application. On these accounts, representation is usually defined in terms of democracy, and limited to a narrow role within democratic theory.

Instead, we want to define representation in its own terms, which means exploring not just its non-democratic but also its non-political uses. But at the same time, we want to argue that representation is the key concept for understanding the workings of modern, democratic states. In making this case, we will be drawing an explicit connection between the variety of uses to which the concept of representation can be put and its particular usefulness in the construction of the most durable and powerful political institutions of the modern world. The central role that the concept of representation has played in our politics is in large part a result of its inherent flexibility. Representation is able to accommodate the range of different perspectives that all modern states must contain and to do justice to the political conflicts that can result. This book aims to show how this came about, what makes it possible, and what might follow from it both now and in the future.

Structure of the book

The book is divided into three main parts plus an epilogue, each of which emphasizes a different aspect of the concept of representation: its history, its internal logic, its political consequences, its potential future. The parts can be read separately but they deal with many overlapping themes and it is only when these are taken together that a full picture of the concept of representation emerges.

The first two chapters explore the historical origins of representation and its evolution into a distinctively political concept, allied to a distinctive political institution, the modern state. In these chapters, we identify the different non-political sources of the concept of representation (in law, religion, theatre) and the different ways that the concept was used to underpin the development of various social and political associations (churches, cities, parliaments). We also emphasize how representation came before democracy in the history of modern politics. The story we tell is therefore not of the emergence of something called 'representative democracy', in which democracy is the foundational idea, and representation simply the qualification. Rather, it is the story of the ways in which democracy has qualified the underlying basis of representative government.

The next two chapters are primarily analytical and examine the many different ways in which it is possible to conceive of the representation first of individuals, and then of groups. The representation of groups can be understood as an extension of the representation of individuals but, as we try to show, it can also generate its own dynamic and its own particular problems, many of which are of crucial importance for politics. The source of some of these problems are best explored by looking at various legal or economic models of representation, which highlight the difficulty of fixing the relationship between the individual and the group. Among the themes we discuss in these chapters are how different models of representation impact on questions of personal identity, of group rationality, and of collective responsibility. These are difficult topics, and nothing about the representation of groups is straightforward. As a result, chapter 4 in particular contains a small amount of technical material related to the problems of collective action. We have tried to make this material as accessible as possible.

The final two chapters develop these themes while also introducing some normative considerations. We explore a number of issues in contemporary political theory and contemporary politics, relating first to the representation of the state, and then to representation in international politics. Various forms of international representation, particularly those involving non-governmental organizations, suggest that we may be moving beyond the state as the primary locus of representative politics. At the same time, various important ethical questions, concerning for example the representation of the global poor, suggest that we *ought* to be moving beyond the state. Yet it is far from clear that representation beyond the state can compete with the distinctive forms of representation that states are still able to offer, and we discuss the reasons why this might be so.

In the light of the resilience of the representative state, we consider in an epilogue one of the most important questions of all: How might the future, including the future of the planet itself, be represented within the politics of the present, and with what prospects of success? This is a pressing question, and it is ultimately *the* pressing question, running throughout the book, about the spatial and temporal limits of representative politics.

Terminology and types of representation

Many writers about representation offer typologies of the concept, in order to distinguish between its basic different forms. The terminology of these typologies tends to vary. So does the number of types for which they allow. For some authors – notably Hanna Pitkin, who remains the most influential writer on this topic – representation essentially revolves around a set of binary distinctions. The most basic of these is between 'substantive' and 'formal' representation, which leads to a distinction between representation as *acting* for and representation as *standing* for (Pitkin 1967). Within each of these categories, there are then further distinctions to be drawn, for example between 'independent' and 'mandated' ways of acting for others, or between 'symbolic' and 'descriptive' ways of standing for them.

Other writers prefer to use three-way distinctions, separating out, for example, 'enactive', 'interpretive' and 'simulative' representation – or, to put it another way, representation as 'instruction', representation as 'interpretation' and representation as 'replication' (Pettit 2006). Alternatively, it is possible to divide representation up according to the different non-political idioms in which the concept originated: here, the significant distinction is between 'juridical', 'theatrical' and 'pictorial' versions (Skinner 2005).

In this book, our preference is for the three-way rather than the two-way distinctions. To put it at its simplest, our basic division is between these three types of representation:

1. Representation where the representatives are told what to do.
2. Representation where the representatives decide what to do.
3. Representation where the representatives copy what to do.

However, nothing is quite so simple. One complication is that in different contexts different terminologies are better equipped to capture these distinctions. So we borrow from a number of different terminologies throughout the book –

including Pitkin's, Pettit's and Skinner's – as appropriate. A more significant complication is that none of these different types of representation is self-contained: each is capable of blurring into the other. To take just one example: it is perfectly possible to instruct representatives to decide for themselves how to act. This immediately blurs the distinction between types (1) and (2). Equally, various concepts cut across the distinction between these different forms of representation. 'Trust', for instance, is often identified with models of representation in which the representatives exercise their own judgement in how to act (this is particularly true when representation is described in the language of 'trustee-ship'). However, trust is an issue in all forms of representation – we need to trust those we instruct to act for us, and people may be more likely to trust representatives who resemble them in important ways. Trusteeship also blurs the lines between the different idioms. It is an essentially legal idea and derives from juridical uses of the term; but it borrows much from theatrical conceptions of representation, in which it is the job of the representative to bring whatever is being represented to life.

However, more important than these potential overlaps is another feature of representation that we emphasize through-out this book: any conception of representation, of whatever type, is bound to contain within it tensions that allow it to be deployed in different ways. These tensions derive from the gap that must always exist between the representative and the represented, no matter how closely one might try to tie them together. If there were no difference between them – if representative and represented were identical – then we would not be dealing with representation but with mere presenta-tion, or simple acts of display. The tensions inherent in the concept of *re*-presentation can be characterized as a kind of paradox – the paradox of simultaneous presence and absence – which is how they were described by Hanna Pitkin (Pitkin 1968). Alternatively, they can be traced back to limitations of a more practical nature, such as the unavoidable asym-metries of information, time lags and breaks in communica-tion that must lie between representatives and those whom they represent. Either way, representation should be under-stood as a concept that not only has a variety of different forms, but in all its different forms is capable of various different emphases. The question is whether this inherent ambiguity is a weakness or a strength. Some political theorists assume it must be a weakness, because it introduces ambiguity to the heart of politics. But in this book, we try to explain how it might also be a strength because of the way it allows certain questions to remain open, or at least to be answered in different ways, depending on what is required, and by whom. This is an openness that is central to the competitive, reflexive and fluid nature of any democratic polity and it suggests that, without representation, there would be no democracy at all.

Part I
The History of Representation

1
The Roots of Political Representation

The idea of representation is modern; it comes to us from feudal government, that iniquitous and absurd form of government in which the human species is degraded, and the name of man dishonoured. In ancient republics and even in monarchies, the people never had representatives; the very word was unknown.

Jean-Jacques Rousseau

Representation is everywhere in the state of society. Before the representative system there was nothing but usurpation, superstition and folly.

Abbé Sieyès

Sieyès was right: representation is everywhere in modern societies. It permeates our everyday lives to such an extent that we hardly notice it. Our innermost thoughts are made up of representations of the external world; the language we use consists of words that serve to represent those thoughts; works of art and other images are able to represent all the things that human beings are capable of imagining, including ideas that we cannot put into words. Representation also functions on a more practical level: actors represent characters on the stage, lawyers represent their clients in court, agents represent their employers in business transactions. Yet none of these forms of representation is distinctively modern; they have all played a part in social existence from ancient times onwards, even if the word 'representation' has not always been used to describe what is going on. What is distinctive about the modern world is the role that representation has played in shaping its politics. All modern states are representative states, in that they are all founded on the ability of their governments to speak and act in the name of the people. There were earlier intimations of this way of thinking in the politics of the ancient and medieval worlds. But it is only in the modern era that it has become unavoidable as a way of doing politics. It is impossible to conceive of political institutions on the scale and of the power of modern states without making use of the idea of representation.

Yet because representation is so ubiquitous as a concept, functioning in so many different settings, it is sometimes tempting to doubt its continued political significance. Many contemporary political theorists have come to suspect that representation is something of a distraction when thinking about politics. Because it is an idea drawn from outside politics – its origins lie in the worlds of art, law and religion – it is easy to believe that all it can do is open up political theory to the potential dangers and distractions of foreign disciplines. It appears to threaten to turn political thought into literary or aesthetic theory, or alternatively to swamp political ideas in the murky waters of metaphysics and epistemology. As a result, contemporary political theorists prefer to concentrate on the problems of democracy and in most cases have given the concept of representation a wide berth. Some of those who do address representation explicitly have come to the conclusion that it is too vague an idea to make sense of democratic politics (Przeworski 1999, Shapiro 2003). Democracy has the advantage that it is at its origin a purely political idea and, though it may be hard to know how democracy can work in practice, it is not hard to know what the word itself means: it means rule by the people. Representation, even considered purely as a word, seems inherently ambiguous. It implies, simultaneously, a presence and an absence: the presence that comes from being re-*presented*, and the absence that comes from needing to be *re*-presented. Given this indeterminacy and apparent inconsistency, there is a strong attraction in reducing the concept of representation to a purely instrumental role and allowing it to be subsumed into the more tractable concerns of electoral politics and democratic accountability. That, for the most part, is where it exists in academic writing about politics today.

This book challenges this pervading tendency. Its central tenet is that representation cannot be dismissed as an analytical category, precisely because modern politics, including modern democratic politics, would not be possible without it. Indeed, however troubling the idea of representation might be for the clear-cut mind of the analytical political theorist, the truth is that it is its inherently ambiguous character that gives representation the kind of flexibility required to negotiate those areas of modern political life (and they are many) in which two, apparently contradictory, answers are needed to one and the same question. Above all, it was only when the people could be conceived as being *represented* by their governments that it became possible to say that, where the government rules, it is the people who also rule. This is the central insight of modern politics and almost everything else follows from it. It is part of our purpose here to give this insight its proper place at the heart of the story of modern politics and to explore what does in fact follow from it. To do so, it is necessary to examine where the idea of representation came from and how it found its way into politics in the first place.

In telling the early history of a concept as varied and as multiply useful as representation, three significant difficulties must be borne in mind. First, the word and the concept have not always coincided: at various points, ideas that we might recognize as belonging to the sphere of representation have been described by the use of different terms altogether. Second, the word itself has always been very hard to pin down, because it is specifically designed to convey a 'dichotomous meaning' (Pitkin 1967), even when it is being deployed in a practical setting. Third, throughout its history, the concept of representation has been described in a number of distinct idioms, with different implications for how representation should work in practice (Skinner 2005). The main idioms for thinking about representation are as follows:

- pictorial representation, according to which representatives ought to resemble and stand in the place of the represented;
- theatrical representation, according to which representatives ought to interpret, speak and act for the represented, thereby bringing them to life;
- juridical representation, according to which representatives ought to act for the represented, with their consent and/or in their interests.

Each of these conceptions of representation is distinct; yet throughout the long history of the concept they have come together in a range of different combinations and settings, some of which have proved much more durable than others.

For all these reasons, the early history of the concept of representation is complex, and we can only offer the broad outlines here. Nevertheless, it is in the early history of the concept that almost all the ideas which inform modern varieties of political representation have their roots. The setting of the modern state provides the location for the peculiarly durable and effective form of politics that we call 'representative democracy'. But the ideas that have been combined to create that form of politics pre-date the modern state entirely.

Representation in the ancient world

Rousseau, as quoted in the epigraph, was essentially correct when he pointed out that the ancient Greek and Roman republics did not talk about 'representatives' (Rousseau 1997: 114). It is true that many of the important functions of Athenian democracy were performed by individuals or small groups acting in the name of the Athenian people, having either been elected or selected by lot for that purpose (Hansen 1991). But the language of representation simply did not exist to describe these roles: ancient Greek had no equivalent term. The terminology of representation is of Roman origin. However, the Latin verb *repraesentare*, from which our modern word derives, did not initially mean 'to represent' in anything like the modern sense (i.e., of speaking or acting in another's name). Rather, the primary senses of the term were (i) paying immediately or in ready money, and (ii) showing or presenting in person, especially when presenting oneself to or before another person. Hence the underlying idea was closer to our current notion of literal 'presentation' – of giving something an immediate or initial presence – than of '*re*-presentation'. For example, a general or politician who introduced himself before the waiting crowd in Rome was said in the original Latin to 'represent' himself, whereas we would say, in describing exactly the same practice today, that he 'presents' himself before his audience.

Nevertheless, the idea of what we would now call representation, meaning a kind of 'acting for', was already at work in Rome, despite the non-use for that purpose of the word itself. For instance, in Roman law, someone's representative in a lawsuit was variously called his *actor*, *cognitor*, *procurator*, *tutor* or *curator*, though never his *repraesentor*. In Roman political thought, the term that came closest to capturing what would later be thought of as a relationship of representation between different agents was drawn not from law but from the world of the theatre, and in particular the practice of mask-wearing. The language employed to describe this practice was that of the *persona*.

The word *persona* was originally used for the clay, wooden or bark mask worn by actors on the stage, indicating to the audience the character whose role they were playing. The republican political philosopher Cicero (106–43 BC) extended the meaning of the term to include the different personages, or parts, that any one of us sustains in everyday life. Just as actors changed their masks as they played different roles on the stage, so people performed different roles, with specific duties (*officia*) attached to them, throughout their lives. At times, this role-playing took on the nature of a private rehearsal for the parts one might have to play on the public stage. Cicero illustrated this in his *De Oratore* with the example of Antonius, an advocate who prepared himself for an important legal case by acting out the parts of the three persons involved, namely his own, his adversary's and that of the judge (Cicero 1942). Similarly, magistrates, as players of public roles, were expected to bear the person of the city (*gerere personam civitatis*) and to behave appropriately, in accordance with the stringent duties that came with the right to speak and act in the city's name (Cicero 1913).

Meanwhile, in the later Roman period, the vocabulary of representation began to be extended to convey a somewhat different idea, that of giving something an additional or substitute presence by standing in for the thing being represented. In the legal context of the repayment of debts, *repraesentare* came to mean the making good of a sum of money that had been originally promised but had not been forthcoming; that is, of standing in for the original debt. More significantly, the noun *repraesentatio* also began to be used to refer to mental images ('representations') of the outside world, conveyed to the mind by the senses, or conjured up by the suggestive powers of oratory (Quintilian 2001). This internal picturing had its external counterpart in works of art, or likenesses, through which the outward appearance of a person, or an object, was faithfully reproduced, and thereby re-presented to the observer's gaze (Pliny 1952). These images too were called *repraesentationes*. Thus the term came to convey not simply real presence but an artificial presence realistically conveyed by someone or something else.

These different senses of the term 'representation' were deployed in a variety of different settings to convey a broadly similar idea of 'substitution'. But in neither its legal nor its more aesthetic uses was the word connected up with the idea of 'acting for' another person, nor with the notion of 'playing a role'. It was only with the birth of Christianity, and its theological controversies, that the word took on a broader meaning, one that could cover the relationship between entities that did not necessarily resemble each other but were nevertheless capable of taking one another's part. It was here, in Christian thought, that the language of representation came to overlap with the idea of the *persona*, paving the way for a novel understanding of the term: a relationship between 'persons' able to stand in for one another by dint of the bond between them, rather than simply because of a likeness that they happened to share.

The first recorded instance of the term 'representation' being used in this new sense comes from Tertullian (*c.* AD 155–230), a Roman theologian and early Christian apologist, who, in a discussion of the Trinity, refers to the Son as representative (*repraesentor*) of the Father. He also resorts to the language of representation to describe the manner in which Jesus, at the Last Supper, represented (*repraesentat*) his body with the bread (a relation, clearly, that cannot have been founded on mere likeness but on a more complex symbolism). In addition to these theological claims, Tertullian made use of the idea of representation when thinking about the relationship between the church and its members. He uses the verb *repraesentare* to denote the idea that a single and more significant entity can be taken to stand for the many scattered and less important entities that make it up (Hofmann 1974). Here, representation is founded precisely on a notion of difference, or superior capacity. This was the origin of an idea that was to have profound significance in the medieval period: the principle that the leading members (the *valentior pars*, or weightier part) were an appropriate body to represent the entire community and could be assumed to stand in for the people as a whole (*universitas*).

But if Tertullian marks an important shift in the potential political application of the idea of representation, his employment of the term lacks one crucial element that we have subsequently come to associate with it. This is the idea that representatives are able to speak and act for those they represent because they have been specifically authorized to do so. The earliest identification of the concept of representation with the principle of authorization seems to have come from a letter from Pope Gregory the Great (AD 540–640) to a local congregation, in which he reassures them that, through the appointment of a new bishop, 'our authority will be represented by someone to whom we give instructions when we ourselves are unable to be present' (Gregory 1899: 1). Here, then, is a use of the term that recognizably foreshadows its later meaning as a form of political delegation: the representative does not simply embody or symbolize another entity, but acts under instruction. On this understanding, power clearly lies with the represented and not the representative, which is the opposite of what happened when the significant persons in a community were said to 'represent' the whole. But two things are worth noting about this early link between representation and delegated power. First, it remained a relatively uncommon use of the term, compared with its use to denote likeness or some other symbolic connection. Second, this was still power coming down from above: representation was a way for the pope to communicate with his outlying congregations, not the other way round.

Representing the church and representing the city

By the Middle Ages, three competing conceptions of representation had evolved from the ideas described above: (1) descriptive representation or mimesis (in the sense of similar things standing in for each other); (2) symbolic representation or representation as embodiment (as in the greater embodying the lesser); (3) representation as authorization or delegation (Tierney 1983). All of these ideas had begun to play a significant role in the theological and ecclesiological writings of the period. Of these different conceptions of representation, the third was the one with the most obvious connection to legal and political questions concerning the distribution of power. Yet on its own, it was able to do little work and seemed merely a tool of established authority, particularly within the governance of the church, where the first two conceptions played a much greater role. It was only when the concept of representation was brought together with another legal idea, that of the corporation, that its political potential began to be realized.

The legal conception of the corporation provided canon lawyers with a device for thinking about the distribution of power within ecclesiastical bodies and the vexed question of the relationship between their heads and their members (Pennington 2006). For example, when discussing the relationship between a bishop and his chapter, medieval canonists developed the notion of the cathedral chapter as a moral or corporate entity which could be understood as being 'represented' by its head, the bishop. But this was still representation in a symbolic sense only: the bishop was considered able to represent the chapter by dint of being the embodiment of its unity, rather than because the members of the diocese had authorized him to act on their behalf (a bishop's authority, as we have seen, came down from the pope, not up from the local community). A similar argument was deployed to describe the governance of the church as a whole. This too could be imagined as one body, consisting of the entire community of the faithful, of which the pope was the head, and kings, emperors and other rivals for the pope's power simply members. In these defences of papal supremacy, the role of representation was twofold: to emphasize the capacity of the pope to symbolize the unity of the whole church (representation as embodiment) and to draw attention to echoes of that unity running all the way through the governance of the church down to the local level (representation as mimesis). There was no place here for representation as a limitation upon the exercise of power, certainly not so far as the pope's own powers were concerned. These came from God, and were effectively unlimited.

But the idea of the corporation also provided ammunition for those theorists who wished to defend other rulers against the threat posed by the papacy, chief amongst whom was the theologian and Aristotelian philosopher Marsilius of Padua (*c*.1275–*c*.1343), who linked the theory of the corporation with an alternative conception of representation, to argue that political authority should be founded on popular consent. For Marsilius, all legitimate government rested on the ultimate authority of the people – the whole corporation of free citizens, whom he called the *universitas civium* (Marsilius 2005). He described the people in their corporate capacity as 'the human legislator' and claimed it was the consent of this entity that made laws binding. On the question of how the people were to express their consent, Marsilius returned to the familiar idea that the corporate will of the citizen body could be represented by the will of its wisest and weightiest part, the best of its citizens. Likewise, if this select group disagreed among themselves, Marsilius argued that the representative body could itself be represented by its more numerous and more prudent part. This formulation raises the obvious question of whether prudence can always be expected to be embodied in the views of the majority. But Marsilius circumvented this difficulty by introducing an additional conception of representation, one that went beyond mere embodiment and moved towards an idea of delegation. The elected magistrates of the people, he argues, must act as 'the representatives of the whole body of the citizens, and of their authority' (*vicem et auctoritatem universitatis civium repraesentantes*) (Marsilius 2005: 8). Moreover, their election is premised on their competence and of this the people are the ultimate judge.

On Marsilius's account, the people could be represented in this way because they were a person in their own right, with a corporate identity of their own. A similar argument was deployed by the Roman lawyer Bartolus of Sassoferrato (1313–57), who claimed that corporate agency within an Italian city republic belonged to the people themselves, which is what gave them the capacity to be represented by magistrates acting in their name (and what gave those magistrates the capacity to defend the people's political arrangements against anyone who wanted to usurp them). But where did the people's corporate identity come from? For Marsilius, the answer was a mixture of theology and classical philosophy: the people were a corporate entity because God had ordained it and Aristotle had confirmed it. For Bartolus, there was simply no general answer at all – it was partly a question of size, since not all communities qualified as peoples; some simply weren't big enough. In definitional terms his argument was somewhat circular: free peoples had a corporate identity because they were big enough to need representatives, and they needed representatives because they were corporate entities.

But during the thirteenth century another way of answering this question had emerged. Pope Innocent IV (1195–1254), who was also one of the leading lawyers of his age, made the case that corporate agents were simply a species of *persona ficta* – fictitious persons – and that their collective agency did not empower their representatives but was rather empowered *by* them. In other words, the people were not a collective person in their own right and, just like any other disparate and potentially disputatious group of individuals, needed representatives in order to act; without representatives, they were powerless. This made corporate personality a condition of representation, rather than the other way around. And in answer to the question where did the power to represent the people come from if the people were incapable of bestowing it themselves, the lawyers who followed Innocent were ready with their response: it depended on the gift of the law-giver, which in any given case might mean either the emperor or the pope.

So by the fourteenth century, the idea of representation had become bound up with contrasting understandings of the relationship between a group's corporate personality and its capacity to act. For some, group personality was a precondition of representation; for others, representation was a precondition of group personality. But in neither case was the idea of representation a free-standing one: its role depended on its place in some higher scheme of thought, whether legal or theological. Nor did these arguments about corporate personality remain divorced from questions of symbolic representation. Instead, the two became inextricably entwined in the ongoing battle between the supporters and the opponents of supreme papal power (Burns and Izbicki 1998).

The conciliar movement that began towards the end of the fourteenth century drew on the theory of group personality to argue that the unity of the church resulted from the corporate association of its members, not from its subordination to a single papal head. The pope's authority was therefore partly ministerial – it was delegated to him by the congregation of the faithful. But the conciliarists also argued that the faithful needed a representative body of their own to take decisions on their behalf. They identified this body as the general council of the church which they believed could claim final authority in all questions of church governance. The most important of these questions was how to protect the church against the possibility of papal heresy or misrule (Tierney 1982).

In explaining why councils represented the corporate will of the church more reliably than any pope, conciliarists

brought together ideas that were to become of crucial importance for the evolution of secular representative institutions:
the necessity of consent for authoritative jurisdiction; the idea
that representative assemblies (rather than single figureheads)
were the proper locus of collective decision-making; the
notion that the wisest part could represent the will of the
whole (Tierney 1983). We also see here a combination of
ideas drawn from the different idioms of representative
thought: representation as a form of delegation (by now
closely identified with the principle of election, since the
council was composed of elected priests and laymen); representation as symbolism (the council, in its wisdom, symbolized the essence of the wider church); but also, crucially,
representation as mimesis, since the conciliarists claimed that
the council could act as a kind of microcosm of the entire
Christian community, with its diversity of members reflecting
the different parts and classes of the wider church. This last
– the representation of diversity by a diversely constituted
assembly – was something no pope was able to do.

The pope did have the symbolic advantage of the unity of
his person when seeking to represent the unity of the church,
but this line of argument raised serious difficulties too (Paravicini-Bagliani 2000). The physical transience of an individual
pope's body stood in obvious tension with the church's institutional continuity. Nor did popes have recourse to the
institutional devices available to kings, who preserved the
continuity of the state through an unbroken chain of succession ('The King is dead; long live the King'). The papacy was
not dynastic and depended on election by cardinals, leaving
inevitable gaps between one pope and the next. Thus the
device that gave popes some rival claim to legitimacy in the
face of conciliar arguments, the fact of their election, also
served to undermine their claim to embody in their own
person the ongoing life of the church.

The conciliar movement suggested two significant things
about the rapidly emerging concept of representation: first,
that it could be deployed on behalf of the wider community
against the supremacy of its symbolic head; and second, that
on its own this argument was not enough. The apparently
superior 'representativeness' of the general council was not
in the end sufficient to withstand the greater power of

the papacy, and in 1517 conciliarism was finally defeated. The real lesson of this struggle was that the concept of representation could not yet settle political controversies on this scale; all it could do, for now, was to complicate them. Evidence that the concept of representation could be decisive for questions of political authority was only provided in a different, and relatively more modest, setting: not the battle between popes and their councils but between kings and their parliaments.

The rise of parliamentary representation

There are some obvious parallels between the rise of the ecclesiastical conciliar movement and the emergence of secular representative assemblies all over Europe during the thirteenth and fourteenth centuries. The spread of representative institutions in both spheres, religious and secular, was informed by two fundamental principles borrowed from Roman private law (Clarke 1936; Edwards 1970). First was the notion of *plena potestas*, according to which a corporate group could consent to being represented by a proctor with full power to bind its members by his actions. Second, the maxim '*Quod omnes tangit*', according to which whatever touches the interests and rights of all is to be approved by all, through their appointed representatives who bear full powers to act in the name of their constituents. But in the setting of emerging parliaments, these ideas did not operate as a meaningful constraint on royal power. Rather, they made parliaments instruments of royal authority, whereby kings could profitably publicize, elicit consent to and put into practice new measures of government and finance. The primary role of representative assemblies was not to broker consent but to guarantee it, by ensuring that decisions taken at the centre could be reliably translated back to the localities. In this sense, medieval parliaments were more about representing the king to the people than the people to the king. They provided a dependable means, as we might now put it, for the Crown to get its message across.

But parliaments served other functions as well, particularly in England where a number of competing principles beyond the Roman legal ones were in operation (Davies and Denton 1981; Seaward 2006). These included the feudal notion that any political superior, including the king, had the customary responsibility to seek *auxilium et consilium* (aid and consent) from those bound to him when undertaking any enterprise requiring their cooperation (above all, when going to war). At the same time, medieval England had seen the growth of a wide range of local, self-governed communities (counties, towns, boroughs, cities), each of which was endowed with a corporate identity and deemed capable of being represented within a national system of consultation and consent. These local communities had their own models of representation, connected with their use of juries, shire courts and other local assemblies. Finally, parliament's role was shaped by the growing practice of presenting petitions for the relief of grievances to the king and his council (Brand 2004; Zaret 2000). These came via parliament, and led to the development of the practice of common petitioning, or concerted action, by knights and burgesses, often to criticize royal policy. This served to give members of parliament an increasing awareness of themselves as a single body, capable of representing wider dissatisfaction with the state of the kingdom.

Parliamentary representatives throughout the medieval period found themselves pulled in two different directions. On the one hand, the assumption that they possessed 'full powers' to bind their constituents made them vehicles of kingly power; on the other, the traditions of local representation, feudal obligation and collective petitioning gave them an apparent duty to refer back to their constituents before taking binding decisions. The result was that a split emerged within the concept of representation between the authority to act and the need to consult. Though medieval members of parliament were meant to come with *plena potestas*, they often lacked full power to consent on behalf of their constituents without consultation. Indeed, it was common practice for the constituency to issue instructions, though these were mostly limited to issues of local concern; and representatives, in their turn, often felt the need to give an account of their actions to their constituents, in particular if taxation had been agreed to. Yet all the while this demand for consultation was growing, efforts were being made to ensure that members of parliament remained free from external pressures when discussing and voting on major affairs of state. This was significantly helped by the fact that parliament's proceedings remained private, carried out far from the eyes and the ears of the general public.

Medieval parliamentary representation foreshadowed some of the familiar tensions of later forms of representative politics – above all, the clash between instruction and independence as principles of action. But what the medieval parliament lacked was a durable sense of itself as a single representative body, capable of speaking for the nation as a whole. This only arrived during the sixteenth century with the evolution of the idea of the 'king-in-parliament' – the single sovereign body responsible for the making and unmaking of law (Elton 1969). With this doctrine came a new way of conceiving the relationship between parliamentary representatives and those whom they represented. In some respects, the building blocks of this conception were familiar because they drew on existing models of political representation, including those we have already seen at work in the ecclesiastical sphere. What was new was the confidence with which they were expressed and the insistence that parliamentary representation now provided the basis for thinking about political authority as a whole.

The foremost Elizabethan theorist of parliamentary representation was Sir Thomas Smith (1513–77), who saw in the idea of king-in-parliament a symbolic representation of the entire realm. The king was its 'head', and the three estates – bishops, lords and commons – together made up the body of the kingdom. Thus parliament was a political embodiment of the complete realm, symbolizing in miniature form all its constituent parts. As Smith famously put it, 'every Englishman is intended to be there present, either in person or by procuration and attorneys, of what pre-eminence, state, dignities, or qualities whatsoever he be, from the Prince (be he king or queen) to the lowest person of England. And the consent of Parliament is taken to be every man's consent' (Smith 1982: 79).

But if this were true, then representation could not be limited to acting on behalf of those who voted for members of parliament, let alone allowing them to issue instructions. The procurators and attorneys in parliament had also to act for those who were disenfranchised – as the 'lowest' persons of England most assuredly were – and to assume that the interests of all classes could be incorporated with those of the worthiest estates and represented through them. Smith's conception of parliament as 'the most high and absolute power in the realm of England' (Smith 1982: 79), whose acts could be taken to denote the consent of literally every person in the kingdom, was an early version of what would later be called the doctrine of 'virtual' representation, whereby the disenfranchised, despite having no say in who represented them, were still said to be present in parliament. It also marked an important break between the ideas of representation/consent on the one hand and authorization/election on the other.

In his view of parliamentary representation, Smith reserved a special place of honour for the figure of the speaker, who symbolized the voice of parliament itself by acting 'as the mouth of them all' (Smith 1982: 82). This was representation as a form of institutional impersonation: the speaker played the part of spokesperson for parliament by adopting a persona consistent with that role. But in one of the ironies of parliamentary history, it was in the role of speaker that Sir Edward Coke (1552–1634), perhaps the greatest of all English jurists, went beyond the views of Sir Thomas Smith by arguing that within the corporate body of king-in-parliament, its different parts fulfilled different representative functions. Coke drew the distinction as follows: 'That his Majesty and the Nobles being every one a great person, represented but themselves, but his Commons though they were but inferiour men, yet every one of them represented a thousand men' (D'Ewes 1682: 515). On this account, kings and lords were not representative of any identifiable version of the nation because they acted within their own sphere, and on their own behalf. Peers, in particular, owed their presence in parliament to the royal summons, not to election. They were the king's councillors rather than the nation's representatives. Only the commons were properly elected and truly representative of significant numbers of men. This numerical superiority was reason to think that the balance of power within parliament ought to shift from the unrepresentative few to the represented many.

Coke was not alone in drawing attention to the fact that the members of the House of Commons had special claims to represent the people at large. A similar argument was often deployed to resist attempts to curtail the independence of parliament, especially when the freedom of speech or freedom from arrest of its members was threatened. For example, a member of one of Elizabeth's parliaments, speaking on behalf of a colleague who had been arrested, insisted that he should not be held in custody, 'for as much as he was not now a private man, but, to supply the room, person and place of a multitude, specially chosen, and therefore sent [to parliament]' (D'Ewes 1682: 175). The implication here was that elected representatives were 'public' men, in ways that those who owed their place in parliament to an accident of birth never could be. Some parliamentarians were developing very precise ideas of how this representation of a multitude by one public man should be conducted. William Hakewell, who would become an authority on parliamentary affairs, spoke as a young man in Elizabeth's final parliament of his passionate belief that representation was a matter not just of institutional impersonation but of putting oneself in another's shoes. As representative men, he told his fellow members of parliament, 'we must lay down the respect of our persons, and put on others, and their affections for whom we speak: for they speak by us. If the matter which is spoken toucheth the poor, then think me a poor man. He that speaks, sometimes must be a Lawyer, sometimes a Painter, sometimes a Merchant, sometimes a mean Artificer' (D'Ewes 1682: 667). The Ciceronian overtones were clear. So was the threat of more to come – the idea of being a public man was not very far removed from the thought of becoming a republican one.

King vs. parliament

During the first part of the seventeenth century, with the Tudors replaced by the Stuarts, the House of Commons became more and more conscious of its standing as a representative institution with special links to the country at large (Hirst 1975). Its members made increasing play of their concern for the judgement of public opinion, while strategically using the notion of their accountability to those they represented to resist the king's requests for money. But if parliament was showing its growing assertiveness, so too was revealed its obvious vulnerability. It remained an institution to be summoned at the king's discretion and, if the king was unhappy with it, he could simply refuse to call it and seek to raise revenue in other ways. An indication of just how vulnerable representative assemblies were in a world of absolute monarchs was provided in France, where the Estates General was not summoned at all from 1614 until the fateful year of 1789. In England, the hiatus was briefer: Charles I chose to rule without convening parliament from 1629–40. In the meantime, however, the idea of parliament as the mouthpiece of the people, and the defender of its civil and religious liberties, did not go away. When parliament finally returned, the moment had come for a decisive resolution of the question of what it meant to represent the English people.

The Long Parliament (1640–60) rested a substantial part of its case against Charles I on the claim that it was *the* representative of the people of England. Chief among the parliamentary propagandists who sought to flesh out this claim was Henry Parker (1604–52), one of the most original and articulate defenders of the legitimacy of parliament's war with its king. Like many other parliamentarian writers of note (such as Charles Herle, William Prynne, William Hunton), Parker explicitly embraced an 'ascending' conception of politics, according to which all rulers received their powers from 'below' – that is, from the people, by some form of conditional agreement, covenant or trust. The people, as a corporate agent in its own right, was, in Parker's words, 'the free and voluntary *Author*' of monarchs and parliaments, two distinct '*actors*' to whom it transferred the authority to act in its name (Parker 1642b). This transfer of power was but 'conditionate and fiduciary', and any particular magistrate was more or less absolute, as he was more or less trusted. Moreover, between these two fiduciary agents there was an obvious discrepancy in the way in which they could act. Although the king was greater than any particular individual (*singulis major*), he was necessarily less than the whole (*universis minor*), and therefore a mere delegate of the greater body of the people. Parliament alone could claim to represent the whole kingdom and if necessary to act on the people's behalf in order to check the monarch's tendency to despotism or misrule.

This, then, marks a decisive contrast between parliament's 'representative' capacity (and Parker was one of the first people to refer to the individual members of parliament as 'representatives' in their own right), and the mere delegated power of the king. But where did parliament's unique ability to represent the wider community come from? Here, Parker went beyond mere authorization to draw on the idea that parliament also provided a faithful miniature image of the kingdom in its entirety. As he put it: 'The composition of Parliaments, I say, takes away all jealousies, for it is so equally, and geometrically proportionable, and all the States do so orderly contribute their due parts therein' (Parker 1642b: 23). So parliament was not simply an authorized actor, it was also a reliable substitute for the thing it represented. It was not long before this uneasy double conceptualization of parliamentary supremacy encountered its critics. If non-freeholders and 'nine parts of the men of the kingdom' were effectively disenfranchised, how could these persons be said to have conveyed authority to parliament to act in their name? Equally, if even in the most popular state, 'some of the poorer, and some of the younger sort, and women generally by reason of their Sexe are excluded', how could parliament be said to offer a reliable representative sample of the people (Digges et al. 1642: 1)? Coming as they did from the Leveller and Royalist sides alike, these criticisms hinted at the fact that an argument for the inevitable identity of parliament and people was paving the way for a new parliamentary absolutism.

Parker had his answer but it was not one likely to set at rest the anxieties of his opponents. Parliament he claimed was not simply a miniaturized, map-like replication of the people; it was an improvement on the original, transforming the bulky and clumsy mass of the public into a manageable form:

'The Parliament is indeed nothing else but the very people it self artificially congregated or reduced by an orderly election, and representation, into such a Senate or proportionable body' (Parker 1644: 18). As the use of the word 'Senate' suggests, Parker was returning to the familiar idea that a people could be best represented by being represented by its betters, the weightier or wisest part of the community. But Parker also insisted that the people had no independent identity at all except in and through the actions of its representatives. This was the strongest possible version of the claim that there was an indissoluble unity, or self-sameness, between people and parliament. 'The whole Kingdome', Parker maintained, 'is not so properly the Author, as the essence in it selfe of Parliaments' (Parker 1642b: 5). And if parliament was 'virtually the whole kingdom itself . . . indeed the State it self', then it could not possibly be conceived that its judgment in 'matters of State as matters of Law' could ever go against the people's interests (Parker 1642b: 28). Parliament, Parker argued, would never be injurious to itself, which is what made it safe to entrust the representative assembly with essentially unlimited powers. The thesis of the infallibility of parliament soon became common currency in parliamentary writings, making the idea of opposition to parliament tantamount to self-contradiction. 'Their judgment is our judgment', as one defender of parliamentary rule wrote, 'and they that oppose the judgments of the Parliament oppose their own judgment' (Anon. 1643).

To the Leveller critics of parliamentary despotism, this way of thinking had entirely lost sight of the principle of authorization that ostensibly underlay it. Like the parliamentarians, the Levellers endorsed an 'ascending' theory of politics, which meant that only elected representative assemblies could have supreme authority to make laws, appoint magistrates and conduct foreign policy. But since the authority of these assemblies was a revocable trust from the people, their members should be responsive to the people and its interests or risk the withdrawal of their right to act. As Richard Overton put it, with a view to criticizing the increasingly tyrannical rule of the Long Parliament: 'We are your principals, and you are our agents' (Overton 1647). Moreover, as 'representers of *Free-men*', members of parliament 'must be substantial and

real actors for *freedome* and *liberty*, for such as is the represented, such as no other must the figure be' (Overton 1647:
12). Overton's radicalism is shown by the fact that he is
advocating not only a mirroring of persons but also a mirroring of ideas: representation is here conceived as a way of
replicating the principle on which the citizen body is constituted, that of freedom.

For representative assemblies to be fully responsive to the
interests of the electors, new constitutional arrangements
would be needed (Wootton 1991). The Levellers championed
the frequent submission of representatives to the judgement of the people (biennial parliaments), the ineligibility of
MPs to sit in two successive parliaments, an increase in the
numbers in the representative body, and the reorganization
of parliamentary constituencies to reflect the actual make-
up of the population. They also demanded a reconsideration
of the question of who should be entitled to vote. In the
Putney Debates of October–November 1647, these arguments came to a head in a series of discussions between the
elected representatives of the soldiers of the New Model
Army ('the Agitators') and their officers ('the Grandees')
(Mendle 2001).

The Agitators put forward the first recorded demand for
a constitution based on universal male suffrage ('one man,
one vote') which they considered to be a birthright. They
reasoned that anyone obliged to obey a society's laws should
have the right not only to consent to government but also to
participate in its operations by choosing their own representatives. 'The right of every free-born to elect', was how
Captain Lewis Audley encapsulated this principle, drawing
on the age-old maxim that anything 'which concerns all ought
to be debated by all'. The Grandees, who included Henry
Ireton (1611–51) and Oliver Cromwell (1599–1658), held a
much more restricted view of the franchise, arguing that the
representative system had to have a property basis. Giving
votes to the propertyless, they feared, could lead to the aboli-
tion of private property, civil strife and chaos. Sufficient
property was a necessary condition of someone having an
independent will, being a freeman, and casting a vote. The
right of the vote belonged therefore not to the free-*born*, but
the free-*man*, a much narrower category.

In the end, even the Leveller spokesmen at Putney felt compelled to accept some of the force of this argument. Despite insisting that a radical extension of the franchise was necessary to secure 'the poorest he' from the tyranny of the 'greatest he', they came to endorse the disenfranchisement of those living in dependence – women, servants and beggars – in what was to be an electorate made up exclusively of heads of households. Nevertheless, within the ferocious disputes on the parliamentary side about what constituted true representation – and what *mis*-representation, a category that also now came to the fore – a deep gap had emerged between those who identified representation with the rights of the represented and those who identified it with the superior capabilities of the representers. In this sense, representation had become one of the central points at issue in English politics. But it remained unclear what these arguments about representation could resolve in ultimate political terms because too many different conceptions of representation, drawn from the full range of classical and medieval idioms, were still in play. How to understand the concept of representation remained at the mercy of ongoing political disputes, rather than being a means of transcending them.

Representing the state

It is for this reason that the most radical theory of representation from this period comes not from the parliamentary side, but from one of the fiercest and most intellectually sophisticated of its opponents, Thomas Hobbes (1588–1679). Having gone into exile in France to escape the perils of the civil war at home, Hobbes reserved his contempt for the 'democratical gentlemen' whom he blamed for starting the conflict in the first place. His masterpiece, *Leviathan* (1651), a ferocious piece of invective as well as a work of philosophical genius, is the fruit of Hobbes's disgust. But it is also a work that borrows many ideas from parliamentary theorists of sovereignty, most notably in its treatment of the concept of representation, while turning them into something quite new.

This is what gives Hobbes's theory its crucial but deeply ambivalent role in the history of the concept of representation. Almost nothing contained within Hobbes's account is original – like everyone else during this period, his conception of representation is a mixture of ideas drawn from classical, medieval and early modern sources – yet its effect was to transform how the concept might be understood. What Hobbes showed was that representation could provide the foundation for a stable form of politics because it was a concept that might transcend the disputes that were tearing the English state apart. Representation, in Hobbes's hands, turned out to be the idea that could hold the state – *any* state – together.

The building blocks of Hobbes's theory are familiar ones. Like Cicero, whom he cites, Hobbes traces the roots of representation back to the world of the theatre. From there, he says, it gravitated first to the law courts, and then to everyday life, and finally to politics, where a person acting for another came to be called (as the 'democratical gentlemen' had come to call them) 'a *Representer*, or *Representative*' (Hobbes 1996: 112). In this way, Hobbes identified representation with what he called 'personation', the business of playing another's part. But he also employed the concept of representation within a juristic contractual framework where he drew on the legal concepts of ownership and authorization. Representing the words and actions of another person presupposes, for Hobbes, a contractual arrangement (a warrant, licence or commission) whereby the actor (the representative) comes to act by the authority of the author (the represented). But in authorizing a representative to act in his name, the author is also, according to Hobbes, agreeing to 'own' whatever actions are performed in his name. In other words, he has to take responsibility for his representative's actions, 'no lesse than if he had made [them] himselfe' (Hobbes 1996: 112).

Hobbes accepted that authors might make arrangements to limit their liability for the actions of their representatives by agreeing merely to be represented for certain purposes or certain periods of time. But he was also clear that arrangements of this kind were only possible once a state of civil society had been established, since they depended on being enforced by the sovereign. The one relationship that could not by definition be subject to such limitations was the one that established sovereign power itself. The reasons, Hobbes thought, were obvious. First, in the state of nature contracts are not binding because there is no one to enforce them. Second, the sovereign needs unlimited authority to bind individuals to their contracts and offer them the kind of protection that they seek. This, then, gives the sovereign representative a distinctive character for Hobbes: only the sovereign represents unconditionally, by having full power to bind every other individual in the state by his words and actions. And this is what every individual in the state of nature must agree to in creating sovereign power in the first place.

But in so doing, they create something else: a corporate identity for themselves. By giving the sovereign 'the *Right* to *Present* the Person of them all', the multitude of individuals who naturally form nothing more than an unruly crowd, with no personality of its own, turns itself into a real political unity. This is the Leviathan, or what we would call a state, as Hobbes does: 'A Multitude so united in one Person, is called a COMMON-WEALTH, in latine CIVITAS, or STATE' (Hobbes 1996: 120). For the people, as a mere collection of individuals, to become a *people*, in the political sense, they must be represented as though they were a single person. As Hobbes explains, in one of the most significant lines not simply in *Leviathan* but in the whole of modern political thought: 'A Multitude of men are made *One* Person, when they are by one man, or one Person, Represented . . . For it is the *Unity* of the Representer, not the *Unity* of the Represented, that maketh the Person *One*' (Hobbes 1996: 114). The importance of this idea lies in the fact that it makes representation a form of transformation: it is by being represented that the state is born.

There is an element of fiction involved in this creation. 'Fiction', as derived from *fingere*, here both has the sense of shaping, creating and making – the state is, after all, the multitude's own creation and has no powers but those given it – and also the sense that the state is, ultimately, an incapable entity (i.e., a kind of *persona ficta*), needing to be represented in order to have any personality at all. This, like so many of Hobbes's ideas on representation, carries echoes of earlier conceptions, particularly the Roman legal idea of the corporation. Likewise, the full powers the sovereign representative possesses to bind his subjects is similar to the original conception of *plena potestas*. Perhaps more significantly, Hobbes's notion that the sovereign can be identified with the state itself follows closely the ideas of representation espoused by parliamentary absolutists like Parker, while Hobbes's separation out of authorization from instruction has distant echoes of the thought of early champions of parliamentary rule, like Sir Thomas Smith.

Leviathan was designed to be able to accommodate the claims of parliamentary supremacy, not only because Hobbes insists that an assembly, so long as it speaks with a single voice, is able to represent the state as well as a king but because the book was published at a time when the parliamentary side had triumphed in England, and so on Hobbes's account constituted its legitimate sovereign. Yet the real significance of the argument contained in *Leviathan* is that its employment of what had originally been parliamentarian ideas of representation, like its use of earlier legal Roman and Ciceronian conceptions, does not predetermine which side Hobbes is on. In this way, Hobbes was turning the ideas of the parliamentarians back on themselves (Skinner 2005). His account of representation is consistent with the victory of either side (though after the restoration of the Stuarts in 1660 this was something he preferred to downplay). It was meant to be above sides; indeed above politics, understood in any narrow sense. For Hobbes, representation was the thing that made politics possible, by making the most destructive forms of political conflict impossible.

There are hints of this idea in earlier theorists: for example, Bartolus understood the city as a corporation precisely so as to be able to argue that the victory of one side in any civil dispute does not have to lead to the exclusion of the other side, so long as the state's corporate identity is preserved. But there are two big differences compared with Hobbes. First, Hobbes puts representation centre stage, whereas for Bartolus it was an idea he mentions in passing, one among many. Second, Hobbes makes representation a free-standing concept, something that does not depend on some higher authority, not God, nor the pope, nor Aristotle, nor the Holy Roman Emperor, all of whose political authority Hobbes was resolved to destroy. Instead, Hobbes equates representation with political authority itself and grounds it on a secular conception of reason and equality (the equality that all reasoning creatures share) (Pettit 2007). Once representation was understood in these terms, then a whole new world was possible.

2
Representation vs. Democracy

The legacy of *Leviathan*

The use Hobbes made of representation in *Leviathan* marks a decisive moment in the evolution of the concept. He freed the idea from its medieval moorings and made it the basis of a distinctively modern theory of politics: secular, rational and transformative. But in closing down the medieval and early modern disputes about representation, Hobbes opened up a potential new source of political disagreement. This is because the lessons that could be drawn from what Hobbes had achieved pointed in two very different directions – one reactionary and one revolutionary. It was the struggle between these two ways of thinking about the concept that shaped what representation was to become – an idea that seemed to stand in opposition to genuine democracy, and yet one that turned into the vehicle of democratic politics throughout the world.

Hobbes had made it absolutely clear that representation was an instrument of power. He showed how the politics of popular consent could produce an absolute obligation to obey if representation was understood in the terms of 'authorization' and 'ownership': when a sovereign representative acts on our authority, we own whatever he does and are bound by its consequences. This made representation a very rigid process in which nothing was allowed to intrude on the ability of the sovereign to impose his will on his subjects, simply by dint of being their representative.

Yet at the same time, Hobbes's theory of representation was not rigid at all because it opened up the possibility that the people could be represented in all sorts of ways that did not require their explicit consent. By making political rule dependent on the representation of a kind of 'fiction' – the fiction of a 'people' in whose name political decisions could be taken even though they lacked the capacity to take decisions of their own – Hobbes cleared a space for new ways of thinking about politics. In particular, he raised the possibility that otherwise unwieldy political units – multitudes of individuals on the scale and of the diversity of the populations of modern states – could still impose their collective identity on the political life of the nation, if only they could find representatives willing to act for them. This was a revolutionary idea and it was to have revolutionary consequences. How people reacted to Hobbes depended on whether they saw the creative potential in his theory of representation or only saw what Hobbes wanted them to see: its absolutism.

Many thinkers who read Hobbes recoiled, unsurprisingly, from the idea that to be represented was merely to be subject to the absolute will of another person. John Locke (1632–1704), for example, did not believe it made sense to suppose that individuals would choose to swap the uncertainties of the state of nature for certain domination by a 'sovereign representative' in the Hobbesian sense (Locke 1988). All legitimate political authority, Locke stressed, must rest on the rational consent of individuals, and what any of us will rationally consent to is limited by what each of us has a right to – our lives, our liberty and our estates. Locke grounded his own conception of representation on the principle of consent and, because consent operated at a number of different levels in his theory, so too did the idea of representation. Consent was required: (1) at the inception of a legitimate state; (2) whenever anyone, by implicit or explicit consent, became its member; (3) whenever the members of the state chose representatives to give consent on their behalf; (4) every time these representatives voted, giving their consent through the voice of their own majority. Thus on Locke's account it was possible for individuals to be represented by others at many different points in the political process, and at some points it was essential.

The purpose of this overlapping scheme of consent/representation was to set limits to arbitrary power, by making government impositions – particularly the imposition of new taxes – impossible without 'the Consent of the Majority, given either by themselves or their Representatives chosen by them' (Locke 1988: 362). This, then, was representation couched in the language of opposition to arbitrary rule. Moreover, if men had the right to choose representatives, to give consent in their name, governmental action either lacking the consent of these representatives or interfering with it could be legitimate grounds for active resistance. Power was in Locke's terms *entrusted* by the people to the prince for the advancement of their welfare. Therefore, whenever magistrates forcibly took the people's property (lives, liberties and estates) without their consent, or whenever they dismantled, or interfered with, the established machinery for choosing representatives, this constituted a serious breach of trust which absolved people from obedience. Ultimately, the notion of consent, channelled through the principle of representation, implied a right of resistance.

But although Locke's version of representation sounds much more forward-looking than Hobbes in this respect, and clearly foreshadows later 'democratic' modes of representative politics, in one crucial respect Locke was going back to the past. He did not resolve the question of what was to *count* as 'consent', tacit or explicit, to the ongoing activity of government. Did consent require the performance of actions which signal a positive assent, such as voting, or was it merely a disposition manifested by certain kinds of behaviour, perhaps including simply living in the commonwealth and abiding by its laws? Because he could not provide a definitive answer to this question, Locke leaves it uncertain as to when the conditions of consent can or should be met by representatives that individuals have not chosen for themselves – that is, when it would be sufficient to rely on what would later be called the condition of 'virtual representation'. Nor does Locke give us clear reasons as to why the consent of the majority should pass for the consent of the whole. Here, as elsewhere, he seems to assume the very thing that needs to be demonstrated – that the voice of the majority speaking for everyone is legitimate in a way that is capable of rendering other forms of representation illegitimate.

Thus Locke had no explanation for how the people might have arrived at the principle of representation in the first place. He simply believed that it was somehow 'natural' that government should be limited in this way, and that agreement about when and how the people should be represented would follow from that. The genius of Hobbes's account was that he did not assume that there was anything natural about representation, nor did he believe that agreement about representation could precede government. He identified representation with the creation of government itself, which he understood as a wholly artificial process. 'Artifice' for Hobbes did not have any of its later connotations of narrow, cramped pretence. It meant creativity, the ability of human beings to fashion a world that worked for them. In this respect, Hobbes's was the more radical account of representation: by making representation co-extensive with the capacity of government to act, rather than a limitation on that capacity, he allowed it to be whatever political representatives wanted to make it.

Someone who recognized the radicalism of Hobbes's thought was Jean-Jacques Rousseau (1712–78). It was not enough, Rousseau saw, simply to go back to some natural conception of representation in order to knock the sharp edges off Hobbes's account of power. Instead, if the unpalatable consequences of Hobbes's theory were to be avoided, Rousseau decided that the language of representation had to be repudiated altogether. He shared with Hobbes the conviction that government was an add-on to the natural relationships that existed between human beings, rather than some kind of extension of them – it was, in other words, wholly artificial. What was crucial for Rousseau was that individuals should not become divorced from the thing they had created. Representation constituted just such a divorce by taking the creative power of politics out of the hands of those who had generated it and lodging it with a separate representative agency: a set of phoney actors appropriating our collective identity whilst, at the same time, claiming to be merely speaking in our name.

It was, for Rousseau, no coincidence that the concept of representation had its roots in the idea of 'mask-wearing', and Rousseau himself extended his rejection of representation to include a rejection of theatrical life in general, which he believed offered only the illusion of true feeling, manipulated to reconcile the audience to their lack of a genuine understanding of their predicament in a 'civilized' society (Rousseau 2004). Morally, the theatrical experience was passive and sterile: it required nothing but surrender of one's judgement. Likewise, political representation was just an act, offering the illusion of true freedom, while manipulating the audience of citizens to conceal their true predicament from themselves. In voting for their representatives, the citizens thought themselves free; in fact, they were enslaving themselves to the will of others: 'The instant a People gives itself Representatives, it ceases to be free; it ceases to be' (Rousseau 1997: 115).

So, for Rousseau, the evolution of the concept of representation had not obviated the need to choose between popular and autocratic forms of political rule but had simply thrown that choice into starker relief. In the end, the choice was one between representation and democracy. As he put it in a letter to Mirabeau of 1767: 'I see no tolerable mean between the most austere Democracy and the most complete Hobbism' (Rousseau 1997: 270). Rousseau did not repudiate Hobbes entirely; indeed, he was profoundly influenced by Hobbes's thought, particularly by his ability to conjure a collective identity for the state out of the natural equality of the individuals who constitute it. But what Rousseau could not abide was the idea that this was nothing more than a kind of conjuring trick, leaving the collective life of the state dependent on being animated by the actions of its representatives. As he made clear in *The Social Contract*, the fact that the state was an artificial entity emphatically did not make it some kind of fiction. He believed that a true political community – one that truly instantiated the freedom of its members – had to be a real person in its own right, with a will of its own. This was the 'general will', and it could not be represented. 'The will does not admit of being represented,' Rousseau wrote, 'either it is the same or it is different; there is no middle ground' (Rousseau 1997: 114). For Hobbes, it was only by being represented that the people could acquire a will. For Rousseau a people who had its will represented was no people at all. It is here that the gap between Rousseau and Hobbes appears unbridgeable.

So it is one of the deep ironies in the history of political thought that perhaps the single most consequential account of the concept of representation was one that sought to combine Rousseau with Hobbes. Its author was the Abbé Sieyès (1748–1836), a one-time cleric who had long since abandoned any interest in God. Sieyès was concerned entirely with politics and the question of how to enable a Rousseauan politics to function in a society that was shot through with relations of representation. Sieyès saw representation every-where: in commercial exchange, where individuals are forever relying on others to do for them what they cannot do for themselves (in this sense, representation was intimately related to the division of labour); in families, where parents take decisions on behalf of their children; in education, where knowledge is pursued by some for the sake of others; and in politics, where Sieyès shared Hobbes's basic insight that the populations of modern states are too large and too individu-alistic to act collectively except through representatives appointed for the purpose. But Sieyès did not agree that the populations of modern states lacked any unity at all without representation. Here, he sided with Rousseau and argued that any state worthy of the name was constituted by a people with a will of its own. Certainly, he believed that the people of France – its 25 or so million inhabitants at the end of the eighteenth century – were a political unit in their own right. He called this unit 'la nation', and he insisted that it was only the nation that could give political representatives the author-ity to act.

Sieyès, therefore, offered a curious, almost paradoxical account of political representation. On the one hand, it was only representation that made national politics possible at all (this was Hobbes). But on the other, it was only the political will of the nation that made representation legitimate (this, in a twisted way, was Rousseau). The nation needed representatives in order to be able to act. Representatives needed the nation in order to be entitled to act. It was out of this apparent paradox that Sieyès fashioned the vision of politics that set the French revolution in motion.

Representation and revolution

In the winter of 1788–9, Sieyès published a series of pamphlets in which he applied his conception of political representation to the travails of the French state (Sieyès 2003). He argued that the Estates General, summoned by Louis XVI in 1788 to sort out his imminent bankruptcy, and divided as tradition insisted between the three estates of the realm (clergy, nobility, people), could not represent the nation. These three estates, separated by the privileges that were available only to the first two, lacked any real unity, and Sieyès was not alone in suspecting that the kind of decisive action needed to resolve the crisis would prove beyond them. But where Sieyès went further than anyone else was to insist that the solution to this problem could not be achieved by extending political privileges to the third estate. Sieyès believed that there was nothing that could be offered to the people by their rulers that they did not already possess for themselves. The third estate – the people – *were* the nation, for two reasons: first, they produced everything of real value (the clergy and nobility, by contrast, were mere parasites); second, they were constituted on a principle of natural equality (the clergy and nobility were nothing without their privileges). So, Sieyès concluded, the only people who could legitimately claim to act for the nation as a whole were the representatives of the third estate. And, in large part inspired by Sieyès's advice, this is what they did: in the spring and early summer of 1789, the representatives of the third estate in the Estates General reconstituted themselves as a National Assembly and set about the business of drawing up a new constitution for France.

Sieyès justified this revolutionary act by means of a distinction between the different capacities in which political representatives could act. In a constituting capacity – that is, as the authors of a new constitution – the representatives in the National Convention spoke for the nation and sought to embody its will in their decisions. They did not do this by consulting with the people, since it was their job as representatives to give the will of the nation political form and in that sense there was nothing with which to consult. But nor did they make the crude Hobbesian assumption that the nation had no will until they had given it one. Instead, they tried to make sure that the constitution they drew up reflected the fact that the French nation was a pre-existing political unit, and should be represented accordingly. This meant that the representatives empowered by the constitution to take future legislative and executive decisions were to do so in the name of the French people as a whole, and not of some part or subsection of them. However, it was crucial for Sieyès that this further class of national representatives – what he called the 'constituted' powers – was not in a position to alter the constitution itself. Its job was rather to represent the nation in specified governmental roles and, although elected by the people, it was not to be instructed by them in how to act – its members were, in Sieyès's words, to be 'true representatives, not mere vote-carriers' (Sieyès 2003:12).

Unfortunately, the actual historical sequence set in train by this conception of representative politics did not follow the pattern Sieyès had in mind. The National Convention never managed to agree, despite Sieyès's best efforts, on a constitution that could stick (and Sieyès, in proposing ever more elaborate constitutional arrangements, did not always help). In the absence of an agreed constitution, the representatives in the National Assembly came to assume more and more executive powers for themselves, in ever-decreasing circles of representation, until the ability to speak for the nation came to reside in just a handful of individuals. From there, it was a small step to a kind of parody of the Hobbesian state, in which sovereign power rested with self-proclaimed representatives of the people, who took it upon themselves to decide who belonged and who didn't, and used the power of the state to enforce that decision in blood. This was the opposite of what Sieyès had intended, as he repeatedly made clear. He had foreseen ever-widening circles of representation, grounded in a constitution which carefully delineated all the ways that the nation could be represented in different capacities – judicial, administrative, military and so on. But in the chaos of the Terror and what followed, Sieyès's attempt to hold the line between the constituting and constituted powers was futile and he, like everyone else, was swept along on a tide of desperate measures and emergency decrees. As the man who had done much to unleash this tide, he was held responsible by many for the destruction that followed.

Yet if one looks away from the historical turn of events, and focuses instead on the core of what Sieyès was advocating, then a different connection suggests itself. The conception of political representation that Sieyès espoused in 1789 had more fundamentally in common with what was happening on the other side of the Atlantic than it did with what was going to happen in France. The basic tenets of Sieyès's view were these:

- Representation was not a second-best form of government to democracy, and should not be understood as merely a compromise forced on us by the practical difficulties of governing in the modern world.
- Representation was consistent with the principles of democratic equality but free from the pitfalls of democratic government; as such, it was a marked improvement on democracy, and its obvious merits served as a rebuke to the palpable defects of crude democratic politics.
- Representation made possible the government of very large political communities without alienating their populations but also without being subservient to them.
- It did this by giving individual citizens the chance to participate in the election of the nation's representatives but not the ability to tell them what to do.
- Because political representatives were free to make their own decisions, it was also crucial that there should be a 'separation of powers' in order to prevent too much power falling into a single set of hands.

- This could be achieved in two ways: by distinguishing between the representatives of the people whose job is to draft a constitution and the representatives whose job is to enact it; and, within the constitution, by distinguishing between the powers of the different branches of government.

All this was precisely what the American Federalists believed as well. Moreover, it was what they, unlike Sieyès, managed to put into practice, via the Constitutional Convention that took place in Philadelphia in 1787, at which popular representatives, elected for that purpose, drafted a constitution away from the prying gaze of the people who had elected them; via a constitution that accumulated vast powers in the hands of the nation's representatives but then carefully separated it out between them; and via a series of brilliant defences of that constitution, the *Federalist Papers*, which explained that the merit of this new system of representative government was precisely that it made popular rule possible on a 'continental scale', while ensuring 'the total exclusion of the people, in their collective capacity, from any share [in the government]' (Madison 2005: 341).

Inevitably, there were significant differences between the authors of the *Federalist Papers* (Madison, Hamilton, Jay) and a thinker like Sieyès. The Americans were not so much influenced by Hobbes and Rousseau, but more by Locke and Montesquieu (though both of these were very important for Sieyès too). This meant that the defenders of the American constitution were much less keen than Sieyès to deploy the idea of a represented 'will' to describe the fundamental character of the new state. The American Federalists were also federalists, even if in some cases (notably Hamilton's) somewhat reluctant ones, and they allowed for a separation of powers vertically – between the national government and the individual states – as well as horizontally. Sieyès was fundamentally opposed to localism and sought to redraw the boundaries of local government in France in order to make it clear that all authority derived from the centre. But the real differences between them were contingent, rather than fundamental. The American experiment in representative government came at the right time, after their revolution was successfully concluded and their unwanted kingly ties disposed of. In France, Sieyès had to try to get his constitutional schemes off the ground in a country just at the beginning of its revolutionary upheavals, with a king they didn't know what to do with, and hemmed in on all sides by enemies who wanted to destroy them. By the time the king was dead, and their external enemies engaged with, the revolution had acquired a life of its own, and was no place for experiments in the theory of political representation.

Two other factors served to obscure the overlap between French and American conceptions of representative government during this revolutionary period. One is the argument that took place in the United States between the Federalists and the Anti-Federalists, for which there was no straightforward parallel in France. The Anti-Federalists opposed the new American constitution on the grounds that it mistook what they saw as the central fact about representation, which was that representatives should be like the people they represent: 'The very term representative, implies, that the person or body chosen for this very purpose, should resemble those who appoint them – a representation of the people of America, if it is to be a true one, must be *like* the people . . . They are the sign – the people the thing signified' (Brutus 1985: 124). From this it followed that the American people needed more representatives than the elite few they were allowed by the constitution (particularly in the Senate), elected more frequently and containing a greater diversity of characters, in order to reflect the diverse character of the American people. As Samuel Chase, a Federalist who nevertheless suspected the new constitution of being insufficiently democratic, put it: 'It is impossible for a few men to be acquainted with the sentiments and interests of the US, which contains many different classes or orders of people – merchants, farmers, planters, mechanics and gentry or wealthy men' (Manin 1997: 112). The die-hard Federalists were suspected of favouring only the last category, to which they belonged (and if they didn't, it was assumed that they aspired to).

The Federalists' response was to maintain that they had a very different conception of the 'character' required of political representatives than the Anti-Federalists supposed. Representation, they insisted, depended on the 'virtue' of the representatives, precisely so that they shouldn't be liable to capture by partial interests. The constitution was designed to provide for the American people 'a more perfect union' and its defenders believed that this could only be achieved by representatives willing to look beyond the perspective of different classes of individuals.

The difference between the Federalists and Anti-Federalists is sometimes characterized in the terms of a distinction between 'substantive' and 'descriptive' representation: substantive representation puts the emphasis on the capacity to act, so that representatives should be able to do things for people that they cannot do for themselves; descriptive representation prioritizes the need for representatives to resemble the people they represent, so that such representatives shouldn't do things for people that they themselves wouldn't wish to be done on their behalf. But there is another way to put it: the Federalists were forward-looking about representation, in the sense that they believed it should not be limited by the political or social circumstances that gave rise to it; the Anti-Federalists were backward-looking, in that they wanted representation to be limited in precisely that way. This doesn't mean the Federalists were bound to win the argument, certainly not without a struggle. There is, after all, something counter-intuitive about the idea that limiting the number and type of individuals who might become political representatives was consistent with expanding the means by which the American people could be represented as a whole. But although this conclusion was counter-intuitive, it was hardly new, since it was also the conclusion Hobbes had reached in *Leviathan*.

It was precisely the Hobbesian aspects of the Federalist case that aroused the most suspicion: they were seen, in their apparent elitism, to be flirting with aristocratic or even monarchical forms of representative government. The Anti-Federalists were able to present themselves as anti-elitists, even if most of them stopped short of calling themselves democrats. As a result, the Federalists were forced to emphasize the essentially negative aspects of their under-standing of representative politics – the separation of powers, the constitutional limitations on government, the avoidance of faction, the use of ambition to counteract ambition – in order not to appear as though they wanted to keep the revo-lution turning until it ended up back where it started, in autocratic rule.

This negative emphasis can give a false impression, however. The Federalists did not believe in autocracy but they did believe in the transformative power of representative government, and in the fact that representation was a tool of government, and not simply a device to limit it. They were, at least as much as their French counterparts, revolutionary in their conception of representation.

But that was not the way it appeared to the greatest anti-revolutionary thinker of the age, Edmund Burke (1729–97). Burke's conception of representation cuts across the revolu-tionary politics of the late eighteenth century and offers a very different perspective on what was at stake, one that makes the link between American and French conceptions of representative government much harder to recognize. For Burke, it was precisely the differences between the American and French revolutions that showed just how dangerous it was to get the idea of representation wrong.

Burke's own conception of representation, based on his experiences as Member of Parliament for Bristol, famously contrasted the unfounded expectations of his constituents to be able to dictate to their representative, with the need for a representative worthy of the name to remain independent of them (Burke 1854–6). Burke believed that political represen-tation was a matter of judgement, not will, and representa-tives were better placed than the people they represented to judge what was best. The exercise of this judgement also required the representation of interests on a national level so that disparate local interests could be shaped into coherent government policy. From this it followed, first, that local or sectional interests, though important to any constituency MP (particularly to any MP's prospects of getting re-elected), could not take priority over the representation of the wider national interest; and second, that everyone who shared in that national interest could be represented in parliament, even if they did not actually possess a vote at the constituency level. This was Burke's celebrated conception of 'virtual' representation and it meant that electoral participation was for Burke neither a sufficient nor a necessary condition for being represented at all.

As with Rousseau, the philosophy that underpinned Burke's view of representation had a strong aesthetic component. But whereas Rousseau suspected that representation obscured the truth in the arts as well as in politics, Burke believed the opposite: that the quest for transparency was aesthetically as well as politically misguided. It was a certain obscurity – or as he put it in his early writings on aesthetics, a 'sublimity' – that gave representation its ability to convey a world of feeling and affect individuals by means of sympathy rather than mere imitation. The imitative arts, such as painting, work by resemblance: as Burke understood it, they try to represent 'literally', to offer exact descriptions of the things for which they stand. In so doing, however, they draw attention to their own inaccuracy, as they sketch out a picture of the world that could not possibly capture its actual complexity, nor be suitably affecting. The non-imitative arts, such as poetry, work by substitution rather than resemblance. They do not present a clear idea of things themselves but display instead the effect of such things on our minds.

Burke preferred non-imitative to imitative arts – i.e., poetry to painting – because poetic representation did not aim at accuracy so much as at a deeper truth. Likewise, in politics, Burke favoured a form of representation that acknowledged the deep complexity of national identity by abandoning any attempt to 'reflect' that complexity in its political institutions. Nations for Burke were intricately evolved entities, and something of their essence would always escape the attempt to replicate them at the level of political representation. Political representatives, in this sense, ought to be more like poets, whose 'business is, to affect rather by sympathy than imitation; to display rather the effect of things on the mind of the speaker, or of others, than to present a clear idea of the things themselves' (Burke 1990: 157).

It was from his understanding of representation as a form of sympathy that Burke developed his own sympathy for the plight of the American revolutionaries during the 1770s.

He argued that the idea of a broad national interest that included 'Englishmen' overseas had been gravely damaged by the impositions of the British Crown on the colonists – who were indeed unrepresented at Westminster in Burke's terms, to the extent that all necessary sympathy for them seemed to have ceased. But what he did not accept was that the answer to this was a reform of parliamentary representation so as to allow the Americans their 'own' representatives, answerable to American constituents. Instead, he argued for an extension of sympathy, and a more open-ended, less rigorous definition of what the nation was – something more sublime than mere 'sovereignty' – in order to allow would-be revolutionaries to continue to be represented within it (Burke 1993).

Similarly, it was his deep suspicion of the attempt to introduce excessive rigour into representative institutions that fired Burke's utter contempt for the French revolution. He was convinced that the catastrophic mistake of the French revolutionaries had been to imagine it was possible to draw up a constitution that reflected where power really lay in French society – with the people. For Burke, this simply meant misrepresenting the nature of society itself by reducing it to an aggregation of individuals. From there, it was inevitable that the revolutionaries would have to impose their will back on the people, with violence, in order to get their preferred vision of French society to hold. No amount of tinkering with the constitutional arrangements – and Burke castigated Sieyès personally as the tinkerer-in-chief, with 'whole nests of pigeon-holes full of constitutions ready made, ticketed, sorted, and numbered, suited to every season and every fancy' (Forsyth 1987: 167) – could hide the fact that the representation of the people was a lie. Like all such political lies, it could be maintained not only at the cost of truth but of blood as well.

Yet Burke's very different reactions to the American and French revolutions have served to obscure the obvious similarities between the conceptions of representation on which they drew. Essentially, Burke wanted to contrast pre-revolutionary America and post-revolutionary France. But in the heat of the two revolutions themselves, what emerged was an idea of representation that did not fit with Burke's categories. Both Madison and Sieyès were explicit opponents of the idea that representatives could be instructed by their constituents to act in certain ways; but both also believed that election was a necessary condition of their acting at all. Neither Sieyès nor Madison believed that the representation of the people meant treating them merely as an 'aggregate' (or what Hobbes would call a 'multitude'), yet both also believed that the corporate character of the people could only be constructed out of the consent of its individual members. Both were deeply sceptical of the idea that 'sympathy' could suffice for representation; yet they each also acknowledged that politics was impossible on the grand scale unless representatives were able to make independent decisions for themselves.

It is true that Sieyès ended up devising increasingly complex and arcane constitutional schemes that made it easy for Burke to parody him as a kind of rationalist gone mad. However, he did so not because he believed that representation should reflect the complex nature of society but because he believed that representative politics was itself a complicated business, requiring carefully calibrated structures in order to ensure that the corporate character of the state should not be dissolved. It is also true that the relative simplicity of the American constitution meant that it acquired over time the kind of sublime and almost mythical character that Burke believed lay at the heart of any stable political society. But neither the complexity and eventual chaos of the French experiment, nor the simplicity and eventual success of the American, should detract from the fact that, both in France and in the United States, the most radical theories of representative politics were seeking to avoid the kind of choice that Burke wished to preserve: an essentially pre-modern choice between aristocratic and popular politics, or between the 'virtual' and the 'actual'. For Sieyès and Madison, representative government was neither popular nor aristocratic. Nor was it either 'virtual' or 'actual' – it was both, in that it derived from the participation and consent of individuals but did not seek to represent them simply as individuals; rather, it sought to represent them as members of the state as a whole.

Representation and the rise of democracy

By the beginning of the nineteenth century, the three major states of the Western world – Britain, France and the United States – had all conducted large-scale experiments in the modern forms of representative government. But in neither their theory nor their practice could any of these be called far-reaching experiments in democracy. In all three cases, the system of government was deliberately insulated from popular control and divorced from the classical principle of democratic equality – the idea that individuals should rule and be ruled in turn. Representatives, even if lacking any class-based privileges, were still a class apart: they were separated out from the body of the people and entrusted with specific decision-making powers. The least democratic of these systems – Great Britain, with its strong monarchical and aristocratic elements and its very limited franchise – had also proved to be the most stable, having endured in a more or less consistent form since 1689. The most democratic – revolutionary France, with its sweeping attack on privilege and its strong popular element – had proved to be the least stable and had reverted in quick succession from Terror to Napoleonic autocracy to the restoration of the Bourbons. Yet notwithstanding these differences, democratic pressures in all three countries now started to grow, raising fundamental questions about whether representative government could, and should, be democratized.

Some of the strongest intellectual pressure for democratic reform came in Britain, where the obvious absurdities of the franchise provided a rallying point for radicals determined to rethink the principles of political representation. The utilitarian movement, under the intellectual leadership of Jeremy Bentham (1748–1832), had long considered the representative institutions of the British state to be a byword for inefficiency and stupidity. Bentham himself had been inclined to believe that reform was best achieved not from below but from above, by encouraging the political elite to listen to enlightened opinion (i.e., to him). It was only when he realized that the British political establishment was not willing to listen to reason that he adopted the more radical idea of pushing for franchise reform – including universal suffrage, annual parliaments and secret ballots – in order to effect change. But throughout his life Bentham remained suspicious of the idea of representation, believing it to be part of the problem, not the solution. He recognized the inherent ambiguity in the principle of representative government which appeared to offer a permanent invitation to independent action on the part of the representative, no matter how wide the franchise nor how regular the elections. As a result, Bentham preferred to talk of 'deputies' instead of 'representatives', in order to make it clear that government ought to be the business of functionaries whose personal qualities were irrelevant.

It was Bentham's friend James Mill (1773–1836) who made the case, against Bentham's better instincts, that representation itself was the appropriate vehicle of democratic reform. Mill's argument, in his *Essay on Government*, was a comparatively simple one. He claimed that the end of good government was to promote the interests of the people; that the danger of all government was that those entrusted with power would abuse it, in their own self-interest; and that representation provided the solution by ensuring that the interests of the community and the interests of the representing body would be the same. Representation did this not by assuming that the representatives were of some higher moral calibre than the rest, but the reverse; that is, by assuming that representatives were just like everyone else and needed to be checked to ensure that their personal interest did not take priority over the community interest. This could be achieved by an open franchise and regular elections which would guarantee, first, that those chosen shared the interests of the community they represented and, second, that they did not have sufficient time to develop a separate political interest of their own. Alternative systems of representation, Mill believed, including those which sought to represent the people in their various 'classes, professions and fraternities', would serve only to create a 'motley Aristocracy' by reinforcing the discontinuity between the representatives' interests and the interests of the people as a whole (Mill 1992: 34).

However, Mill's argument contained two substantial flaws, both of which were mercilessly exposed by Thomas Macaulay (1800–59) in the *Edinburgh Review*. First, Macaulay pointed out the tension between Mill's claim that representation entailed an identity of interest between government and people, and his simultaneous supposition that all political representatives, however chosen, will have a tendency to act against the popular interest and must therefore be restrained. Either representation presupposes an identity of interests or it threatens it – it cannot do both. Second, Mill's argument for an extension of the franchise stopped short of including women, on the grounds that women, like children, could be regarded as having an interest entirely bound up in that of their fathers or their husbands, so that 'the aggregate of males, of an age to be regarded as *sui juris* . . . may be regarded as the natural Representatives of the whole population' (Mill 1992: 27). In so claiming, Macaulay points out, Mill 'placidly dogmatizes away the interest of one half of the human race' (Mill 1992: 291). If 'natural' representation is allowed here, relying on a principle of 'sympathy' between the sexes and excluding actual participation, why, Macaulay asked, is it forbidden elsewhere, in the relations between political representatives and those whom they represent? Mill had no answer. It was a mistake his son, John Stuart Mill, made sure not to repeat.

Reform of the franchise arrived in Britain in 1832, nine years after Mill's essay first appeared and three years after Macaulay's riposte. It was much closer to what Macaulay than Mill had in mind: piecemeal, gradualist and firmly based on a property qualification for the franchise, such that the 'virtual' representation of the bulk of the population still massively prevailed (the franchise was extended from 435,000 to 652,000 in a population of 24 million). Such gradualist options were not available in France, where no scheme of representation had remained in place long enough to be steadily reformed. There, the pressures for a new democratic conception of political representation were founded on the traumatic experiences of the revolutionary and post-revolutionary period, during which it became clear just how detached the interests of so-called 'representatives' of the people could become from the people they ostensibly represented. As Benjamin Constant (1767–1830) put it in 1815: 'All the constitutions which have been given to France guaranteed the liberty of the individual, and yet, under the rule of these constitutions, it has been constantly violated. The fact is that a simple declaration is not sufficient; you need positive safeguards' (Constant 1988: 289).

For Constant, the only true safeguard was the vigilance of the people themselves, communicating with and passing judgement over their representatives in order to forestall the abuse of their powers. Again, this communication did not entail instruction or mandate but rather what Constant called 'surveillance'. Borrowing an image from Sieyès, he described the relationship between the represented and their representatives as akin to that between busy individuals and their business managers: 'Rich men hire stewards' (Constant 1988: 324). While a relationship of this kind would be rendered self-defeating by constant interference – the point of having a steward was to save yourself the time and trouble of endless decision-making – so also would it be crazy simply to trust in the steward to look after your affairs. Rich men who do not keep an eye on their stewards soon become poor. So Constant championed wide citizen participation in politics (albeit one founded on a property qualification), not merely by voting, but by ongoing critical judgement, expressed through petitions, newspapers, debating clubs and so on. This conception of politics can be construed as a democratic one – it is what Pierre Rosanvallon has recently called 'negative democracy' (Rosanvallon 2006). As such, it is democracy founded not on trust in representation but on mistrust, tending towards the formation of interest groups organized around the politics of resentment, and on protest as a semi-permanent form of political expression.

The democratic pressures on representative government that existed in the United States were different. They were primarily social in nature. The social order that emerged from the revolution was a decidedly democratic one, with considerable economic mobility and a widespread assumption that one man's interests were as good as anyone else's (Wood 2003). The framers of the constitution had both assumed and feared that the political expression of this democratic ethos was likeliest to be found in the House of Representatives and their constitutional arrangements, including an electoral college to insulate the presidency from popular majorities, were designed to safeguard against this. Yet it was in fact in the office of president that the democratic impulses of American society first found a national political voice. The crucial year was 1828, when the election of Andrew Jackson heralded the beginning of a period in which it was understood that the president could plausibly claim to represent, both in his own *persona* and in his populist politics, the mood of the national majority.

When Alexis de Tocqueville (1805–1859) arrived in America in 1831, the democratic impulses of American society were immediately apparent to him. So also, though more slowly, did he become aware of the tendencies of the democratic impulse to ally itself with a strongly centralized form of government (something that Jackson, a defender of state rights, had used his popular authority to fight against). As Tocqueville wrote in Volume Two of *Democracy in America*: 'This immortal hatred, more and more aflame, which animates democratic peoples against the slightest privileges, particularly favours the gradual concentration of all political rights in the hands of the sole representative of the state' (Tocqueville 2002: 645). What is striking about this passage is how little Tocqueville believed representation mattered to the inherent tendency of democracies towards tyrannical egalitarianism; all that mattered was the concentration of power itself. Indeed, for Tocqueville, political representation was more or less an irrelevance, since the essence of democracy lay in its social character, while its political character, both in its positive and its negative aspects, was an outcrop of that.

In this sense, Tocqueville was the first of a new generation of democratic writers who treated representation as a byproduct of the workings of democracy rather than the other way round – his interest lay in representative democracy, not democratic representation. The idea of something called 'representative democracy' had first been articulated by Thomas Paine (1737–1809) during the American revolution. Paine did not see representation as a means of escaping cumbersome democracy but instead as a means of enhancing and completing the democratic ideal itself. But Paine's remained a minority view, even among those who shared his revolutionary spirit. For Tocqueville, representation served not to enhance, nor even to modify, democracy but simply to cloak its true nature. In this, as we shall see, he spoke for many political theorists and political scientists to come.

Tocqueville's warning against the possibility of a democratic tyranny of the majority found a strong echo in the thoughts of John Stuart Mill (1806–73). But by contrast with Tocqueville, Mill stands as the last in a line of thinkers who believed that representation could serve as effective insulation against the threat of majoritarian democratic politics, and particularly against what he considered the dangerous American idea that 'any one man (with a white skin) is as good as any other' (Mill 1991: 340). In his *Considerations on Representative Government* (1861), Mill championed a conception of politics that emphasized the capacity of representatives to voice the better instincts of the wider public, by means of their capacity to think for themselves and to exchange their opinions openly, in a parliamentary setting. But deference to the 'mental superiority' of one's representative did not mean total abnegation of judgement on the part of the constituents: if some of their representative's opinions went against their own, 'it is for *him* to satisfy *them* that he nevertheless deserves to be their representative' (Mill 1991: 381).

Parliament as a whole, Mill believed, ought to be a 'Congress of Opinions, an arena in which not only the general opinion of the nation, but that of every section of it' had its cause pleaded and a chance to be heard (or represented) in deliberation (Mill 1991: 282). This required the adoption of a system of proportional representation. Mill wished to ensure that not just the majority but also minority voices were represented, by sympathetic spokesmen, capable of both informed advocacy and deliberative judgement. Were the assembly to be identical with majority opinion, parliament would be incapable of performing its two main functions: first, the *control* of the operations of government, by throwing the light of publicity on its acts; and second, the fostering of an inclusive political *debate*, which is what gives laws their legitimacy in so far as it allows for minority opinions to play a part in the legislative process.

The great danger for Mill was that this openness would be swamped by intellectual mediocrity and the democratic tendency towards the representation of sectional 'interests', which would reduce politics from a free exchange of ideas to a crude negotiation of pay-offs. Interest-based politics would, he feared, lead to class legislation on the part of the numerical majority (i.e., the class of manual workers) at the expense of the public good. In an attempt to prevent all of this, Mill argued for Hare's system of proportional representation, which provided a greater opportunity for minority representation and the possibility that men of talent whose 'constituents' were geographically dispersed could still be returned to parliament. This, he hoped, would limit the power of parties, parochial local candidates and narrow material interests.

Parliament, Mill argued, should primarily represent people, not geographical entities: 'I cannot see why. . . people who have other feelings and interests, which they value more than they do their geographical ones, should be restricted to these as the sole principle of their political classification' (Mill 1991: 318). He also mistrusted any reform of the franchise that continued to distinguish between voters on the basis of an arbitrary property qualification. He wanted reform which assumed that all individuals were potentially capable of participation but which either prevented or limited their participation until they had reached that minimum standard of educational attainment or economic independence which indicated an ability to see beyond their narrow material interests. Votes were to be distributed according to educational and other social attainments, with more votes for 'bankers, merchants and manufacturers' than for 'tradesmen and labourers', and no votes at all for those with no means of supporting themselves. Mill also advocated the opening of the franchise to women, not on the grounds of equality, and not for all women, but precisely because he believed that not all women were equally unsuited to participate in representative government and that some (of the better sort) were at least as well qualified as many men.

The year Mill published his *Considerations* was also the year that the American proposition that all men (with a white skin) were as good as each other was put to the ultimate test in a civil war that eventually led to its repudiation. But of course this was not a repudiation of the assumption of crude equality itself, as Mill might have wished, but rather of a wholly arbitrary discrimination based on skin colour, which Mill saw as the flipside of the absurdity of American democratic egalitarianism. The American Civil War also put to the test the two conflicting aspects of Andrew Jackson's legacy for representative politics: the claims of the executive to represent the nation as a whole and the claims of the localities to be represented against the centre. The war resulted in the triumph of the first over the second. Abraham Lincoln's victory confirmed the ability of a strong president to act as a unifying national representative. Yet Lincoln was not, at least at the outset, a representative of majority opinion. Instead, he was a creature of the party system, and it was only by shrewd manipulation of minority interests within it that he was able to achieve national office at all. One of Mill's fears about the coupling of representation with democracy was that it would make the rise of political parties, pandering to various interest groups, unstoppable. Though he strongly supported the Union side in the civil war, nothing much about the outcome of the war itself served to allay those fears.

Disappointed by the war's aftermath in America, Mill was also to face disillusionment in Britain when a second Reform Act was passed in 1867 which, despite personal misgivings, he felt obliged to support as a member of parliament. His amendment proposing the enfranchisement of women was rejected; and the franchise was extended among men, not, as he wished, on the basis of their aptitude to exercise it but of their rentable income. Moreover, the passage of the Act itself epitomized the way representative politics was going, against principled opinion – Mill lost his own seat in 1868 – and towards the skilful management of parliamentary majorities. The fact that it was a Tory measure, introduced by Benjamin Disraeli to outflank his Liberal opponents, highlighted just how little principle had to do with it. Post-1867 representative politics, in Britain as elsewhere, came increasingly to be identified with the mastering of popular opinion through the regulating device of the newly emerged party machine.

Plebiscitary representation and party politics

When he reflected in 1919 on the rise of the modern political party over the previous century, the German sociologist Max Weber (1864–1920) noted the paradoxical nature of the changes it had effected. On the one hand, party-based representation had made politics more mechanical, bureaucratic and interest-based. Despite this, however, many of the major political parties, particularly in Britain and the United States, had become fixated on the ability of their leaders to reach out beyond a partisan base of support in order to represent the nation as a whole. One early example of this kind of leader cited by Weber was Abraham Lincoln. Another was Disraeli's great rival, William Gladstone. As Weber saw it, these men were not reduced by the partisanship of party politics to its petty level but were empowered by the party machine to transcend it. Political parties needed winners, and winners were almost by definition not simply party hacks. Gladstone, by appearing to step outside and beyond party politics in his Midlothian campaign of 1879–80, had become what Weber christened 'a dictator of the electoral battlefield' – the living embodiment of a novel kind of plebiscitary representative (Weber 1994: 342). His claim to represent the nation derived from his capacity to articulate a personal vision of politics that commanded electoral support in ways that enabled the party machine to throw its weight behind him. As Weber recognized, this potent combination of popular acclaim, professional organization and personal charisma offered representative politicians a kind of power beyond anything seen before.

Was it democratic? The answer to the question depends on whether it is considered sufficient for democracy that the people should simply approve of what is being done in their name. But though its democratic character is in doubt, it constituted a recognizable type of political representation: it combined a capacity for decisive, independent action on the part of the representative with a reliance on the support of those on whose behalf that action was undertaken. Neither the independence nor the dependence could be said to predominate because each was a precondition of the other. This is a conception of representation that stretches back to Hobbes, and Weber gave his own version of it a Hobbesian slant by grounding it in the language of coercion: political representation entailed, among other things, that the representative 'should have at [their] command the material resources necessary to exercise physical force should the circumstances demand it' (Weber 1994: 313). Nevertheless, Weber's was also a post-Hobbesian conception because of its emphasis on the role of electoral competition in ensuring that strong leaders could emerge and weak ones be dispensed with. Weber's great regret was that Germany had failed to evolve a representative system of this type and had been lumbered with too many weak leaders. Though Bismarck had given Germany universal male suffrage, he had also bequeathed it a frail parliament and an electoral system based on proportional representation. The result was that elected representatives, with no opportunity to exercise real power, and nothing to do but worry about re-election, became focused on narrow, petty, partisan politics. Meanwhile, those with the real power – the Kaiser and his unelected ministers – were answerable to no one at all.

For Weber, modern political representation, despite the advances of democracy, was an unavoidably elitist form of politics. Indeed, if democratic representation was to be possible at all – that is, if it was to be compatible with responsible political decision-making rather than simply being a means of avoiding it – it had to have what he called a 'Caesarist' element. Representatives of the people could not simply be *of* the people; they had to be men apart, capable of asserting their personalities in such a way as to win the acclamation and support of the masses. Only such charismatic political leadership could resist the ossification of politics at the hands of growing bureaucratization, party machinery and organized material interests. Weber was just one of a number of early twentieth-century political theorists who had noted the trend towards elitism in representative politics (see Ostrogorski

1964; Michels 1999; Mosca 1939; Pareto 1997). Drawing on a wide body of empirical evidence, they all pointed out that extensions of the franchise, rather than closing the gap between political representatives and those they represented, had served to widen it. Where they differed was in the extent to which they believed this to be unavoidable, and how much they regretted it. Weber did not think it was avoidable and, partly because of that, he did not think it worth regretting much. But what neither he nor the others believed was that the tension between representation and democracy was an illusion – they certainly did not think that the potentially authoritarian and inescapably elitist nature of representative politics was what *made* it democratic. Indeed, it is not clear that anyone really believed this until the case was made during the 1920s by the German jurist and philosopher Carl Schmitt (1888–1985).

Schmitt was a close reader of Weber who shared many of his concerns, particularly about the weakness of systems of proportional representation (Schmitt 1988). Schmitt took these concerns into the Weimar period, where he witnessed what he saw as the inevitable struggles of a state that tried to reconcile a pluralistic form of interest-group politics with the need that all states have for unity, built upon decisive leadership. The great mistake, as Schmitt saw it, was to suppose that pluralism and its associated values and practices were somehow democratic, whereas decisive leadership was not. Instead, he believed that the political indecisiveness and instability on such conspicuous display in Weimar Germany were symptomatic of liberalism. The liberal model of government by discussion – and here Schmitt explicitly had in mind something like John Stuart Mill's vision of free parliamentary debate by independent representatives capable of being persuaded by the best or most truthful argument – had, with the expansion of the franchise, given way to assemblies colonized by party functionaries, organized around deeply antagonistic class-based interests and preoccupied with deal-making and vote-counting. The time had come, Schmitt believed, to turn from the broken machinery of liberal parliaments to a more vital form of democratic representation.

Like Tocqueville, Schmitt thought democracy was *the* modern political principle; unlike Tocqueville, however, Schmitt used this diagnosis to justify the elimination, rather than the application, of a series of liberal restraints on the workings of democracy. Democracy was decisive in its very nature and it needed to be rescued from liberalism if it was to survive. Liberalism privileged heterogeneity, a separation between state and society, the public representation of private concerns and interests, the privatization of politics. Democracy was, by contrast, a quest for homogeneity which rested upon a set of political identifications between governed and governors, the people and their representatives. This meant that democracy could only reveal its decisive character in the modern world through the instrument of representation, which in its true sense stood opposed to liberalism (proportional representation, on this account, was a corrupted, liberal form). True representation meant capturing the essence of the thing being represented and in the case of the people this meant their character as a decision-making entity. In addition, representation bestowed dignity in Schmitt's terms. For the people, it did this by showing them to be capable of sustaining strong leadership by having their political 'essence' and 'unity' embodied in a single authoritative representative. 'The idea of representation,' Schmitt wrote, 'is so completely governed by the conception of personal authority that the representative as well as the person represented must maintain a personal dignity – it is not a materialist concept' (Schmitt 1996: 17).

It was not a large step from here to a celebration of plebiscitary forms of representation more or less detached from electoral competition altogether. So in 1926 Schmitt wrote: 'The will of the people can be expressed just as well and perhaps better through acclamation, through something taken for granted . . . than through the statistical apparatus that has been constructed with such meticulousness in the last fifty years' (Schmitt 1988: 16). In 1933, he took the personal step of joining the Nazi Party, believing Adolf Hitler to be a representative politician who had been legitimized by popular acclaim, not just by mechanical vote-counting. Eventually, Schmitt came to see that he had been wrong about Hitler – after the war, he claimed that he had misjudged Hitler's true character, thinking him to have been a simple dictator, when he turned out to be a totalitarian thug. But he was wrong about representation too. His mistake had been to collapse the distinction that Weber had always upheld between the mechanical and the mystical dimensions of political representation.

For Weber, although plebiscitary leadership was necessary to compensate for the formal legalism of modern rational government, it could not simply be collapsed into arbitrary rule. The charismatic ruler must remain committed to an 'ethic of responsibility', which required him to account rationally for his motives, and to estimate the consequences of his actions (Weber 1994). It was the job of parliamentary democracy to ensure that no leader could forget these constraints. For Schmitt, an anti-parliamentary Caesarism was truer to the essence of political experience as 'a pure decision not based on reason and discussion and not justifying itself . . . and absolute decision created out of nothingness' (Schmitt 1988: 66). Weber believed modern representative politics included both a rational and an irrational element, embedded in the bureaucratic organization of the mass party and the charismatic personality of the plebiscitary-democratic ruler respectively. These elements could not be reduced to each other, yet nor could they exist without each other. Schmitt, in his dismay at what he saw as the creeping encroachments of liberal materialism in Weimar politics, tried to extricate representation from its rationalizing elements altogether, returning it to its early theological aura, and its deeply personalist roots. That is why Schmitt ended up with Hitler whereas Weber had started out with Gladstone.

Another close reader of Weber, the Austrian economist Joseph Schumpeter (1883–1950), made a mistake that went in an entirely different direction. Schumpeter agreed with Weber that democratic politics was inevitably elitist but he abandoned the idea that representation could be a means of bridging the gap between the elites and the rest. Instead, spurred on in part by the terrible misjudgements of people like Schmitt, he dismissed entirely the idea that the people could be represented in a way that corresponded to their will, or their essence. This was because, Schumpeter insisted, they possessed no will or essence of their own. They were just a crowd of individuals.

Democracy for Schumpeter was simply a competition among elites to secure the consent of the wider public to govern them, something that was bestowed periodically through elections. But Schumpeter's error was to identify the concept of representation exclusively with the inflated notion of democracy that he was trying to debunk – absurdly, he associated the idea that the people's will could be represented with authors like Rousseau (Schumpeter 1976). He failed to notice that the modern conception of representation has its roots in Hobbes, who shared his scepticism about the ability of crowds of individuals to act with a single will but saw representation as part of the solution rather than part of the problem. Because Schumpeter regarded the representation of the people as a hollow idea, he came to treat representation itself as an irrelevance: just one of the terms people use to conceal from themselves the true nature of democratic life which was nothing but competition for power. So where Schmitt had tried to collapse democracy into representation, Schumpeter chose to discard the concept of representation altogether.

Democracy vs. representation

Unsurprisingly, of these two followers of Weber, Schumpeter's sceptical view of representation has proved much more influential than Schmitt's fantastical one. For many political theorists today, it remains the case that representation is a distraction when thinking about democracy – it simply sets up false expectations. As one prominent contemporary Schumpeterian has put it, representation is 'an inescapably suspect idea' and should be approached with great caution when considering the basic principles of democratic theory (Shapiro 2003). Within rational choice theory, representation also tends to get treated as something of an irrelevance since the problems of aggregating individual preferences into collective judgements hold for representative assemblies as much as for any other kind of ostensibly democratic body. For this school of thought, representation does not solve the problems of democracy; it merely replicates them.

Some contemporary political philosophers have found a place for representation within their conceptions of democracy; this too, however, tends to be in a narrowly instrumental role. For John Rawls, the idea of representation was primarily located within the context of the 'original position' through which the hypothetical judgements of rational persons are taken to represent the considered judgement of society as a whole (Rawls 1999). When it comes to the business of applying these judgements to the real world rather than within a hypothetical setting, followers of Rawls generally take it for granted that the essential character of democratic justice is unaffected by the fact that it is exercised through the institutions of representative government. Representation, on this account, is a device but never a principle of just political action. Similarly, the recent generation of deliberative democrats, inspired in large part by Rawls and Jürgen Habermas, have sought to reform or to bypass conventional representative institutions by grounding politics in a more explicitly democratic framework of values: openness, communicativeness, reasonableness (Habermas 1984; Rawls 1993). Representation may serve these ends, if it is conducted in the right way – there can be open, communicative, reasonable forms of representative politics. But representation is only of value in so far as it does serve these ends. In chapter 5 we will look at some exceptions to this rule but generally speaking representation is defined and defended within contemporary political theory in the terms of democracy, rather than the other way around.

In this sense, contemporary political thought – whether scientific or philosophical – echoes Tocqueville. It treats democracy as the founding principle of modern political life and representation as the appendage. Depending on whether it is the sunnier or the bleaker aspect of the Tocquevillian legacy that comes through, representation appends democracy either by being one of the instruments of practical politics that must be judged according to democratic values, or one of the essentially empty ideas that are used to conceal the true nature of democratic tyranny. The widespread use of the phrase 'representative democracy' reflects a general sense that, for better or worse, political representation is nothing without its democratic underpinnings – that without democracy, representation is just a word.

Yet as we have seen in this chapter, Tocqueville's understanding of the relationship between democracy and representation is the exception rather than the rule in the modern history of the evolution of these two concepts. The dominant tradition, which runs from Hobbes through thinkers as various as Sieyès, Madison, Constant, John Stuart Mill and Weber, takes representation to be the essential idea and democracy, at best, to be the qualification. The thought that unites this dominant tradition is that representation contains within itself both democratic and non-democratic elements and, far from presenting us with a choice between them, it presents us with the resources that obviate the need to make such a choice. The concept of representation is what allows for creative thinking about how to combine popular participation with the necessary detachment on which all viable forms of modern politics depend. As a result, there are good reasons to doubt that what has emerged from this tradition is best described in the prevailing terminology of representative democracy; rather, it is a world of more or less democratized forms of political representation. Representation remains the foundational idea of modern politics in ways that contemporary political theory has often missed or chosen to ignore. We need to recognize that modern politics has always been, with respect to the central place of representation within it, a recognizably Hobbesian enterprise.

Nevertheless, in one important respect, Hobbes got political representation fundamentally wrong. In his obsession with order, and in his desire to bury the medieval tradition, he assumed that all viable representative bodies had to follow the model of the state (he even argued that families were like mini-states, to be represented by the sovereign head of the household). The opposite is true: there are many other ways of thinking about representation than those described in this chapter, which have been concerned exclusively with representation at the level of the state. There is local representation, and personal representation, and commercial representation, and cooperative representation, and much else besides. All of these different forms of representation play an important role in the life of modern states, in ways that Hobbes either missed or deliberately ignored. Moreover, some are much more democratic than others. The next two chapters of this book will explore these different varieties of representation in order to get an alternative perspective on the problems of representative politics. The approach will be analytical rather than historical, looking at the full range of models for which the concept of representation allows. Only then will we be in a position to return to the question of the state and to ask how far the story of democratic representation that runs from the seventeenth century to the twentieth is likely to continue into the twenty-first.

Part II
The Logic of Representation

3
Representing Individuals

The history of representation makes clear that there is no single underlying model of the concept that was subsequently developed or elaborated to produce more complex versions. If anything, the reverse is true. Representation began life as a complicated, multifaceted idea that has been progressively pared down by political theorists searching for a clarified understanding of what it can do. But a historical perspective is not the only one available for thinking about how representation might work. An alternative approach is to start with what are analytically the simplest models of representation and then to see what can be built on top of them.

The simplest models are those that involve the representation of individuals by individuals, each treated as separate agents. This chapter explores a range of these different models of representation, drawn from sources that prioritize the experience of individual agents. This means borrowing conceptions of representation that are most often seen at work in economics and law. The aim is to get a clear understanding of the different ways that the concept of representation can be used. This analytic approach connects with the various modes of representation that we have seen at work in the history of the concept – representation as authorization, representation as trusteeship, representation as identity. But it separates them out to explore them in their own terms. We then go on to ask in the following chapter what work each of these conceptions is able to do in the more complex setting of group activity that provides the basis of all politics. In this way, it is possible to explore whether the idea of representation can be rescued from its messy history and instead organized around a series of more durable conceptual distinctions. Some of these distinctions might then provide the basis for a normative account that shifts the focus away from what representation has become and towards what it ought to be. This is the subject of the final part of the book.

Representation as a principal–agent relation

The simplest standard model of what is involved in representation is one that follows the principal–agent format (borrowed from private law and commonly used in economics, though as we have seen the terminology itself stretches all the way back to the Leveller debates of the 1640s). The most straightforward version of the principal–agent relation sees individuals hiring other individuals to do some job for them that they cannot do for themselves. Here, one person (the *principal*) appoints another (the *agent*) to perform some action or function on their behalf. Often, the action will be specified in advance so that the agent will be acting within narrowly defined limits. However, it is also possible to have a principal–agent relationship defined in very broad terms, giving agents considerable latitude in how to perform their role (this is sometimes referred to as 'agency slack'). Either way, what distinguishes principal–agent relationships is the understanding that the primary purpose of such an arrangement is to uphold or further the interests of the principal. As a result, representation understood in these terms tends to focus on the interests of the represented and it is a model of this kind that tends to be preferred in accounts of political representation that focus on the interests of the voters.

However, even in the simplest forms of principal–agent relationships, there are a number of different factors to be taken into account. First, the relationship does not necessarily run in a single direction – that is, from the interests of the principal to the actions of the agent. Instead, the relationship can run in two directions: from principal to agent, establishing what the agent is authorized to do, and from agent back to principal, establishing what responsibility the principal bears for the actions of the agent. It is this second feature of principal–agent relationships that brings them under the heading of representation. For example, if I hire someone to mow my lawn, I am the principal and that person is my agent. But someone who mows my lawn is not necessarily my representative. If they fail to mow my lawn properly, then they will have failed me as a principal, and I will have to bear the consequences; but it does not follow that I will have been misrepresented by their actions. Representation requires something more than an agent acting under instruction for another's benefit; it also requires that the principal is somehow implicated in what the agent does. For principals to be represented by the action of an agent, they have to have a *presence* in the action itself.

Yet it is precisely because principal–agent relations are organized around the interests of the principal that it can be tempting on this model to try to define the idea of representation solely in terms of interests and to ignore the question of presence. If someone fails to uphold my interests, we will often want to say that the individual concerned has failed to represent me properly. So if I ask the person who is mowing my lawn to take the mower in for repair and fix a fair price with the repairer, only to discover that he or she has agreed an inflated price and pocketed the difference, I will be entitled to say that my agent failed to act as my representative. But there are three important things to remember here. First, my interests being at stake is not sufficient for something to count as an act of representation. We often act in other people's interests without representing them – giving money to someone who is destitute and begs for help will invariably be in that person's interests but it does not make you his or her representative. Second, it would be a mistake to elevate selflessness on the part of agents into a necessary condition of representation. No agent is ever entirely selfless. Even the person who negotiates a fair price for the repair of my mower will be thinking about themselves at some point (how long will this take? will it lead to more work?) in a way that will impact on what is considered fair. Third, it is still possible to represent other individuals while acting against their interests. For example, a lawyer who makes a mess of a case is still representing his/her client, even though the client would be better off had he or she been represented by someone else. Lawyers only cease to represent a client when the client sacks them. Acting in someone else's interests is therefore neither a necessary nor a sufficient condition for something to count as an act of representation.

It is my *presence* in the action of someone else – the fact that another person is not merely trying to help me but is acting *for* me – that allows me to call that person my representative. As a result, in relationships of representation the question of how a principal might seek to control the actions of an agent is always an issue. There are different ways in which principals can try to control the agents who represent them – that is, there are different ways for them to assert their presence. One method of control is to give agents clear instructions about what they may do. But another is to insist on tight limits to the responsibility a principal bears for what is actually done. If I hire someone to represent me in a business transaction, I might explicitly instruct my representative to negotiate on my behalf only within certain financial limits. Alternatively, I might say that I will only bear responsibility for any agreement that is undertaken on my behalf if it falls within those limits. The aim in both types of cases is the same – to ensure my agent does not commit me beyond what I can afford. But the nature of the relationship will be different: in one case I am trying to tell an agent what to do by limiting that agent's personal responsibility; in the other I am relying on the agent's personal responsibility (and the fact that there are various liabilities that I will not honour and so may attach to the agent) to limit what any agent might think it wise to do.

An example like this also illustrates that relationships of representation cannot simply be understood in terms of the arrangements that exist between principals and their agents. There are also the people with whom these agents deal. In a business transaction involving an agent acting on behalf of a principal there has to be a third party to transact with, and third parties will always want to know exactly how the principal is implicated in the actions of the agent. Even the simplest forms of representation involve the possibility of three separate relationships:

- between the principal and the agent;
- between the agent and the third party with whom the agent is dealing on the principal's behalf;
- between the principal and the third party with whom the agent is dealing.

This is the other distinctive feature of representation: for principals to be present in the actions of agents, they have to be present *for* someone else (this is not the case when my agent simply mows my lawn). As well as principals and agents, representation also requires an *audience* of some kind.

The result is that even the simplest form of representation understood in principal–agent terms are considerably more complex than the simplest forms of principal–agent relationships per se (see figures 3.1 and 3.2). In relationships of representation, principals will need to consider the following questions. How closely are they able or willing to monitor

Figure 3.1 Simplest principal–agent model

Figure 3.2 Simplest representation model

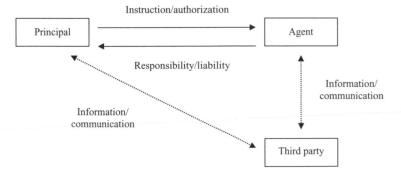

the actions of their representatives? How much congruence is there between the interests of the agent and their own interests? What other factors are likely to influence the way their representatives act? Agents will want to know: what degree of responsibility are their principals willing to take for their actions? What level of scrutiny are they subject to? How clearly defined are their principals' interests? Third parties will want to know, as far as possible, the answer to all these questions because much of their own behaviour will depend on how they understand the respective interests, liabilities and independence of the two parties they are dealing with. For instance, a third party dealing with an agent known to be trusted by the principal might behave very differently from one dealing with someone known to be on a tight leash.

What all parties have to accept is that there will inevitably be some asymmetries in relationships of representation. This is true for even the most straightforward forms of representation, never mind the more complex political models that we will go on to discuss in subsequent chapters. An agent's interests will never coincide exactly with those of the principal because agents are always persons in their own right with interests of their own. Information will also be unequally distributed: principals can never know everything that agents do on their behalf because agents cannot be subject to perfect scrutiny. Likewise, representation can involve significant time lags between actions and their effects so that agents may do something which they believe accords with the interests of the principal, unaware of the ways that the principal's interests have changed. This problem is not what it was – the months and sometimes years that it took for information to travel across the globe in the pre-steam age meant that no one could be sure of what had changed in the interim, whereas information technology now allows for near-instant access to decisions taken anywhere on the planet. But still there will be gaps – representation, by definition, entails an absence as well as a presence, so that what agents do is not always immediately accessible to their principals. Third parties may try to exploit whatever gaps exist. As a result, representation always takes place in circumstances of incomplete information, risk and uncertainty.

Given this uncertainty, perhaps the basic question to ask is why any principal should choose to be represented in the first place. Principal–agent relations imply that principals take a decision to allow someone else to do something for them instead of doing it for themselves. This may simply be a question of convenience – as Constant said, rich men hire stewards. But it might also reflect a judgement on the principal's part about his or her own competence – clients hire lawyers not just for convenience (in fact, the results are often deeply inconvenient) but because they wish to be represented by someone who can do a better job than they could do themselves. These different possible motivations for choosing to be represented by an agent pose different sorts of problems. Expert representatives will have to be given a certain amount of discretion to exercise their own judgement but if they have too much discretion they may lose sight of the interests of their clients. Representatives performing more rudimentary tasks will need to be kept in check to prevent them straying beyond their own competence but if they are subject to too much surveillance then the whole purpose of the arrangement – its convenience – will be lost. In each case, there is a balance to be struck, and how best to do it will often depend on the details of the case itself.

What though of principals who require representation for actions that they *cannot* perform for themselves? Here, it is important to distinguish between two kinds of incapacity. A client might hire a lawyer to act as a representative in a complex legal transaction which in the absence of legal representation simply could not happen because no one would know how to proceed. Although in this case the principal is dependent on being represented for the action to take place, the principal is not completely incapable because he or she retains the capacity to authorize a representative to act (and presumably to fire that representative as well). This is different from cases of representation where the person being represented lacks even the capacity to make such an appointment, as would be true of small children, or other sorts of mentally incapable individuals (including the unborn). What is crucial to recognize here is that in these latter cases we have moved beyond the boundaries of principal–agent relations because the individuals being represented do not have the personal autonomy we expect of principals. This then becomes one of the central issues when considering the applicability of the principal–agent model to politics. As many theorists from Hobbes onwards have pointed out, politics may well depend on the representation of entities, up to and including the state itself, which are incapable of acting for themselves. It is for this reason that the question of how to represent children and other incapable entities is of great potential significance for thinking about political representation.

Hanna Pitkin, who rejects what she regards as Hobbes's unacceptably paternalistic conception of political representation, argues that children cannot be represented because representation entails a capacity on the part of the represented to object to what is being done in their name (Pitkin 1967: 162). She classes children along with inanimate objects and other abstractions as entities that can be represented symbolically or figuratively – in the way that a country can be represented by its flag – but not substantively, since substantive representation depends on individuals being able to assert their presence in the actions of their agents. Of course, it is still possible to take decisions on behalf of children and indeed their incapacity often makes this essential. But Pitkin is keen to ensure that the language of representation does not become too promiscuous in accommodating incapacity because she fears this will allow the representatives of capable individuals to ignore their wishes. To put it at its simplest, Pitkin is fearful that if we allow loose talk about the representation of children, then political representatives may treat the voters they represent as no more capable than children of knowing what is best for them. And this is precisely what Pitkin thinks that the Hobbesian conception of representation is ultimately offering us.

There is certainly something to be said for trying to limit the scope of representation to cases where it is possible to object to what is being done on another's behalf. As we have already seen, Pitkin is right to insist that merely acting in another's interests is not sufficient for something to count as representation. Parents who feed their children every day are acting in the children's interests but are not representing them. This is not simply because the action is unobjectionable. It is also because there is no context in which it would make sense for the child to assert a presence in the action of the parent – to whom would this presence be asserted, and to what purpose? What is missing here is an audience.

But it does not follow from this that there are no cases in which someone acting in a child's interests can be said to be representing that child. Parents who speak on behalf of their child at a school meeting – perhaps to complain about the way the child is being taught – can plausibly claim to be representing their child by looking out for its interests. One reason this fits the criterion of representation is that there is someone to whom the actions are addressed – the parents are defending the child's interests in a context where that interest needs to be made present before an audience (in this case, the teachers and other parents). But what still seems to be lacking is some limitation of any parent's capacity to usurp their children's interests in the act of representing them. What if the parents are wrong about how the child is being taught (the teaching is excellent) and wrong to complain about it (their proposals would make things worse) but the child is unable to say this because the child is presumed not to know its own interests? Do we still want to say that the parent is representing the child? And if so, do we risk turning the parent into a kind of Hobbesian mini-sovereign?

Clearly, by this point we have moved well beyond the framework of principal–agent relations. We have also moved from purely descriptive to semi-normative questions of what should count as representation. The difficulties arise because it is no longer clear who is principal and who is agent – the child ought to be principal if being represented but the incapacity of children reduces them to a passive role, allowing the parent to initiate as well as enact the role of representative. The attraction of viewing representation in principal–agent terms is that it rules out these sorts of ambiguities. But it remains a relatively narrow framework, precisely because it cannot make sense of the representation of people and things incapable of representing themselves. To make sense of this sort of representation, it is necessary to introduce another legal model: trusteeship.

Mandate vs. trust

The idea of representatives as trustees acting on behalf of individuals who cannot act for themselves has often been used to supplement principal–agent conceptions of representation. Trusteeship does not always presuppose incapacity on the part of the person being represented – for example, a simple form of trust would be one that placed the property of a responsible adult in the hands of a trustee because the original owner is abroad or otherwise cut off from the day-to-day management of their affairs (the management of the estates of the original Crusaders fell under this heading and was an early version of a kind of trust). This sort of arrangement is not so different from hiring a steward. But the significant legal difference is that trustees do not simply manage someone else's affairs; for the duration of the trust, they actually own the property in question (this is what makes it a question of 'trust' because the property has been handed over). For this reason, it is possible to argue that trusteeship in its strict legal sense should not be classed as a form of representation at all. Trustees are not acting for other individuals but acting as owners of property that has been passed to them for a certain period. The beneficiary to whom the property will revert bears the consequences of what the trustee does but is not necessarily implicated in the trustee's actions. Trustees are, in this respect, their own persons.

Nevertheless, it is not hard to see why trusteeship should offer a compelling metaphor for certain kinds of representation. This is because trustees are meant to act in the interests of their beneficiaries when transacting with third parties, despite having the discretion to exercise their own judgement. Trusteeship offers a contrast with the model of representation that sees representatives as acting under instruction. This is often called the 'mandate' model. Mandated representatives act as mechanical, passive extensions of their principals – they are a kind of megaphone through which principals make their voice heard, and they are required to keep checking with their principals that they are saying the right thing. The trouble with this sort of model of representation is precisely that it is so mechanical and, if it is meant to be an arrangement of convenience, it risks becoming deeply inconvenient. Trustees, by contrast, are more flexible because they do not act under direct instruction from the individuals whose interests they are upholding. Instead, they are empowered to do what they think best.

But another advantage the trustee has over the mandate model is that it can be extended to cover the representation of individuals who cannot act for themselves. Trustees often look after the property of individuals who are beneath the age where they can look after it themselves and this can be extended to individuals who remain unborn, enabling trustees to protect the property for the benefit of future generations. If trusteeship is understood as a form of representation, then it seems to provide a basis for thinking about how incapable entities can be represented. But it only does so by introducing a fourth party into relations of representation – the capable individuals who set up the trust in the first place. Trustees who act for children, for instance, are authorized by the individuals who appoint them to be the child's representative. Here, trustees are bound not by the instructions of the person they represent but by the expectations of the person who establishes their power to act. In the case of a parent establishing a trust for a child, the model would look like figure 3.3.

In the case of legal trusts, however, all these relationships would themselves be founded on the relation between the individuals concerned with a particular piece of property. So the underlying picture looks like figure 3.4.

Figure 3.3 Simple trustee model of representation

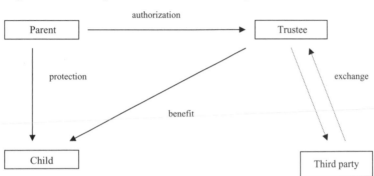

Figure 3.4 Model of legal trusteeship

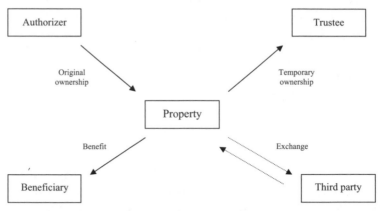

A model of this kind requires the enforcement of the courts to uphold the property relations on which it depends – in early English law, trusteeship evolved as the specific responsibility of the Court of Chancery. But once we view trusteeship in these terms, it starts to look less attractive as a model for representation. Chancery was the setting for Jarndyce vs. Jarndyce, Dickens's metaphor in *Bleak House* for the nightmarish complexity and inefficiency of the English courts in dealing with the property of minors. It's not hard to see how things might go wrong here – a conception of representation that introduces four separate claims on individual pieces of property could take a lot of disentangling. At this point, straightforward paternalism might start to look more appealing.

What though if we move beyond the strict legal model and replace the idea of property with the broader notion of interests? It is often said that trustees are meant to represent the interests of beneficiaries. What this means is that trustees should bear these interests in mind when they undertake transactions with third parties. Another way to put it is to say that the interests of the beneficiary should be present in these transactions. But we are still faced with the question of how that presence is to be understood. There are a number of difficulties here. First, interests, unlike pieces of property, are not an objective category. Different parties are likely to disagree about whether or not particular interests are present because they are likely to disagree about what those interests actually are. Second, it is not clear how an arrangement of this kind can be established if the beneficiaries are incapable of acting for themselves. What is to substitute for the idea of 'original ownership' if this is no longer to be a relationship based on property? Third, in the absence of legal enforcement, what is to prevent trustees from abusing their trust and simply failing to bear the interests of the beneficiary in mind?

All of these difficulties relate to the same problem: how can the presence of the beneficiary be asserted in the actions of the trustee so that their relationship can be understood as one of representation rather than merely a case of one person looking out for another's interests (as when a parent looks after a baby)? On the principal–agent model, principals can assert their presence by objecting to what the representative does on their behalf. For Pitkin, this capacity to object is a necessary condition of all forms of legitimate representation. In the case of trustees, the gap between original ownership and eventual benefit in the underlying model seems to rule out this possibility because the individuals who might object are not the individuals whose interests are being represented. But if we adapt Pitkin's argument and say simply that it is a necessary condition of this form of representation that *someone* should be able to object to the way a representative is acting, then the problem becomes less acute (see Runciman 2007). Take, for example, the case of a parent authorizing a trustee to look after the interests of a child. The child can't object to what the representative does but the parent can. Indeed, when parents do object, they are likely to couch their objection in the terms of representation, viz. 'You were meant to be representing my child's interest, but you have just been looking out for yourself.' It is this element of contestation, as we shall see in chapter 5, that ultimately proves vital to the adaptation of this model of representation to democratic politics.

The result of this contestability of claims to represent is that trustee models of representation, unlike principal–agent models, leave open the question of whose objections are going to prove decisive. When an agent acts for a principal, then it is clear that the principal's objections must be decisive. If a lawyer wishes to plead guilty on behalf of a client who objects and insists the plea should be not guilty, the lawyer has no choice but to acquiesce (even though the lawyer may think, with good reason, that a guilty plea is in the client's best interests). But in the case of trusteeship, the incapacity of the persons whose interests are being represented to object on their own behalf means that others may compete for that role. This may not seem to be an issue in the case of parents who appoint representatives to act for their children because parents might be said to have 'original ownership' over their children's interests. It would take a brave person to tell a child's parents that their objections to what a representative is doing in their child's name are not decisive (though when the child's interests are at stake, bravery may be just what is required).

But in parent–child relations, there is the further problem of knowing what to do when parents establish themselves as the representative of their child's best interests. Let's return to the case of a parent seeking to represent a child by complaining about the teaching at a school meeting. On the account given above, *someone* needs to be able to object to what the parent says if the child is to have some presence in the action. If parents can say anything on behalf of their children (for example, that as the child's representative, they have decided to cease educating that child altogether) without anyone else intervening, then it is hard to see how that child's interests are being made present because it is not clear how the child's interests are to have a presence independently of what the parent happens to be saying. But if a teacher can object to what the parent is saying, by stating that it is not in the child's interests, then we can plausibly think of this encounter as falling under the heading of representation because the child's interests are being treated as having some independent existence apart from the claims of the parent.

What remains to be resolved, however, is the basis of the teacher's claim. Do teachers have some better understanding of children's interests than parents? Or has someone appointed them to speak up for the child in this particular case? Either way, the ability of any teacher to gainsay the parent will depend on their being able to show that they too are a plausible representative of the child's interests. This is the central difference between representation as a principal–agent relation, and representation as a form of trusteeship. In the case of the first, any tension derives from the different perspectives of the representative and the person being represented. In the case of the second, the tension derives from the rival claims of different representatives to identify the best interests of the represented.

To summarize: trustees may be thought of as representatives if there is some way of making the interests of those whom they represent present in their actions, independently of whatever the trustees themselves happen to say or do. But there is no simple or knockdown way of establishing that presence, as there is in the case of principal–agent relationships where the objections of the principal are decisive. In this chapter, we have deliberately avoided any extended political examples because we want to clarify the analytical distinctions before moving on to the politics. But to conclude this section, it is worth spelling out the political implications of what has been said here. Trusteeship is often thought of as one possible model of political representation. This cannot be literal trusteeship because literal trusteeship is a property relation upheld by specialized courts of law. It must be a metaphor. But even as a metaphor, the idea has limits. If political representatives can claim to be able to speak for the interests of those they represent without anyone being able to object, then this is not representation but simple paternalism. On the other hand, if the people they represent are able to object on their own behalf, then this is not trusteeship but a principal–agent relationship (which doesn't mean it is necessarily a form of 'mandate', since principals can allow their agents plenty of slack, as we have seen). It is only trusteeship if the representative's claim to act in the interests of the represented is subject to some competing claim from a rival representative – whether a politician, a newspaper, a pressure group, a crowd – which can give those interests a separate presence. That separate presence should never be confused with an objective presence – the claims will always be in competition with each other. How they are settled is the stuff of politics itself, and this is what we will consider in the final part of the book.

Representation as identification

However, there is a third way to think about the representation of individuals that is distinct from the two we have considered so far. Representation understood as a principal–agent relationship and representation understood as trusteeship both entail the conscious decision by someone to *appoint* a representative. They are, at root, legal models and they presuppose fixed arrangements made for particular purposes. But there is another way an individual can be represented by someone else which occurs when an individual identifies with the actions of another person in a way that gives that individual a stake in the other's actions. For example, if someone in my street makes a complaint about noisy neighbours, I may feel that they are also representing me, even though I have not appointed them or instructed them to complain (perhaps no one has). The reason they represent me is that I identify with the complaint because my experiences are similar. They are speaking for me because we have something in common.

There are many different ways that one individual can identify with another, both inside and outside of the scope of politics, and it is important not to assume that these are all forms of representation. A person might sympathize with someone else without feeling that the other person is some kind of representative. If I hear a tale of family woe that reminds me of my own family, I may identify with it (or as people often say, 'relate' to it) but that doesn't mean I am represented by it. This is because representation requires a third party, or audience. If I am simply listening to someone's story, and finding myself in sympathy with it, this doesn't give me an additional presence elsewhere. But if I read that story in a newspaper advice column, and feel that the advice coming back could apply to me too, then it makes sense to say that someone else is representing me. Identification is a form of representation when it gives one person a presence in the actions of another by dint of something that they share.

Usually, what they will share are common interests. People who live in the same street have a shared interest in keeping the noise down, so that when one person complains, he or she complains for everyone. However, what people can also share are accidental qualities, which make it likely that they have interests in common but by no means certain. If I have suffered from a particular form of discrimination, then someone else who has suffered the same discrimination and gone public with their grievances could be said to represent me. This is what we mean when we talk about certain individuals being the 'poster child' for a particular cause. But it does not follow that my interests are being served by being represented in this way – I may find that all the attention being given to one person leaves me worse off than before (for example, it might get in the way of serious attention being given to the full scope of the problem). Having interests in common with someone with whom one identifies becomes even less certain when the basis of the identification is not some shared experience but simply a shared attribute: family, gender, race, religion. We need to be careful not to assume that representation as identification necessarily entails the representation of interests. That is the hope but not always the outcome.

Underlying this hope is the idea that someone who resembles me in important respects will act as I would act and therefore promote my interests automatically. That is the positive version of representation as identification. But there is also a negative version which allows me to identify with people who share in any adverse consequences of the decisions that they take. If the person who sets the noise abatement levels for my street also happens to live in my street, then I can be reasonably confident that any decision will serve my interests because the decision-maker cannot offload the consequences on to me. This form of representation produces a similar outcome to principal–agent mechanisms which require agents to take some personal responsibility for what they do. But it works in the opposite way. Agents take responsibility for their own actions at the point where they cease to represent their principals; as such, representation marks where one set of responsibilities end and another begins. But when we identify with our representative, then representation marks the point at which responsibilities overlap.

The other big difference is that representation as identification does not depend on the consent of the representative. Agents have to agree to act as agents. But I may find myself the poster child for some cause without having any say in the matter. So people can find themselves acting as representatives against their own wishes – women, for example, are sometime told that they speak for other women whether they like it or not. But individuals cannot be represented against their own wishes – here, the point about objections being decisive still holds. If you say or do something with which I identify, then I may consider you to be my representative. But if I say or do something with which I think you ought to identify, your telling me that you do not identify with it is enough to break the ties of representation. Take the example of the noisy neighbours. If I identify with your complaints, then you represent me. But if I don't identify with your complaints (perhaps because noise doesn't bother me, or because I want to be noisy myself), then your telling me that I ought to share your concerns doesn't make you my representative, in the absence of a prior agreement between us. The language of representation is highly flexible but it has its limits and this is one of them.

However, at this point we also clearly reach the limits of what it is possible to say about representation by restricting it to the cases of individuals representing individuals. We also reach the point at which it is necessary to consider some more detailed political examples. As the case of women speaking for other women shows, relationships of identification are not conducted on a one-to-one basis. They also involve groups. Because we never completely identify with another human being – if we did, we would be identical with them – any form of identification will be partial, which means that it is always possible for more than one person to identify with the same individual, and for the same individual to identify with more than one person. Representation in this sense is unavoidably a collective activity. But once we are in the domain of collectives, then a whole new set of questions arise. How should we think about the representation of groups? Are they to be understood as principals, capable of action in their own right, or as incapable entities, and therefore subject to forms of trusteeship, or simply as alliances of like-minded individuals who can be represented by dint of what they have in common? The answers will depend on the types of groups we are talking about and on what we expect their representation to be able to achieve. It will also depend on how we think the members of groups ought to be able to object to the ways in which the group is being represented. These questions are the subject of the next chapter.

4
Representing Groups

In the previous chapter we discussed three broadly contrasting models of one-to-one representation, as well as the main conceptual distinctions underpinning them. As we moved from representation as a principal–agent relation, through representation as trusteeship, to representation as identification, it became clear that we were no longer simply speaking of representation as an individual-to-individual relationship. Representation inevitably tends to become a collective activity, involving sets of individuals, or groups. As such, representation, though it may still be grounded on legal or economic models, becomes unavoidably political.

The necessity for a transition from individuals to groups is hardly surprising. As we saw in the opening chapters, the category of 'representation' was historically central for thinking about how collectives can function and organize themselves in various spheres of life, from religion and business through to politics. The theory of political representation has therefore always applied primarily to groups. For the many advocates of individualistic conceptions of political representation, however, it continues to make little or no sense to speak of representatives as representing groups, if by that we do not mean that they represent the individual persons who compose them. Group representation is therefore often understood in terms of the representation of individuals. The logical implication of this view is that it ought to be possible for individuals within groups to exercise a veto power over the claims of their representatives to represent them. Whenever the actions undertaken in the name of the group face the explicit objection of some of the group members, these may then be able to claim that they are no longer being represented. At this point, the possibility of a conflict between the individual and the group becomes inevitable – whose voice should predominate? The answer to this question depends on a series of further questions. Can groups ever be represented as such? That is, can they ever be represented against the objections of some, or even many, of their members?

This chapter will address these questions by returning to the three basic models of representation developed in the previous chapter as analytical tools. We will be asking if groups are to be conceived as principals, capable of action in their own right, and of appointing, if not always of instructing, their own agents. Or whether they are to be taken as entities incapable of acting on their own, which must therefore rely on trustees for furthering their interests. Or whether many of the groups we encounter are simply sets of individuals, sharing common interests and/or experiences, who are to be collectively represented by people of their own type. These are questions for which, as we will see, there are no universal answers. It all depends on the type of group we are talking about and on what we expect to achieve through its representation. In particular, the category of the 'interest group' is one that can cut across a number of these analytical distinctions.

But besides borrowing analytical tools from the previous chapter, we will need to develop new tools as well. This is because the representation of groups carries problems of its own which cannot be solved by simply looking back to the representation of individuals. Groups are networked collections of individuals. They are plural in nature: no two individuals in a group are the same. Therefore, the discussion of group representation cannot be detached from the question of collective responsibility – whether what is attributed to the group on the basis of the actions of its representative is also the responsibility of all members of the group. Does group representation entail the responsibility of individual members for what is done in their collective name, or does it provide them with a means of escaping those responsibilities altogether?

The answer to this last question depends, again, on what type of group we are considering and on the ways in which objections by group members can be expressed. Therefore, before we move on to the discussion of the first model of group representation, it may be useful to put forward a working definition of the 'group', as well as a basic typology of groups, which provides some background to what follows.

What is a group? For our purposes here, a group can be defined as a collective of individuals who are connected with each other in ways that are relevant to them, and/or others, and thereby affect their behaviour and/or that of others. This interconnection may be of different kinds and may be relevant for different reasons. It may, for instance, mark the group members out in their own perception and in the perception of others, or determine their opportunities, disadvantages and interests relative to other groups in society. Those of a specific racial or ethnic background may constitute a group on this basis, as may those who share a particular profession, social condition or environmental cause. But those who paint their nails the same colour do not qualify as a group: they lack any durable connection or any connection that is of significance.

Broadly speaking, a group can either be voluntary or involuntary, cooperative or non-cooperative, an agent or a non-agent.

- Involuntary groups are groups into which we are born, such as ethnic groups, not ones we choose, or can exit at our own discretion. By contrast, voluntary groups are groups we join by choice and can also leave freely. Examples of these include political parties, advocacy networks, protest groups and various other civil associations.
- Groups can also be divided into cooperative and non-cooperative. Cooperative groups act on a shared intention to promote an agreed end. They are jointly committed to something. In non-cooperative groups, this shared commitment does not exist. The individual group members act each on their own initiative, and for their own ends,

as determined by their various preferences. An ethnically based pressure group, organizing itself around the question of segregation, is an example of a cooperative group. Conversely, a group of stockbrokers transacting business on behalf of their various clients behave as a collection of independent agents, not as a cooperative agency. What makes them a group is the fact that they may pool resources, and share common rules and obligations of that enable them to perform their independent roles more effectively.

* Finally, groups can be agents or non-agents. Groups that are agents distinguish themselves from other groups by their capacity to *act*. They are no mere networked collections of individuals. They are sets of individuals who besides being networked can act in ways that resemble those in which individual agents act. This means that they can define goals for themselves, perform tasks, appoint representatives and be held responsible for what these do on their behalf. Committees, governments, and joint stock companies are groups of this type. At the other end of the scale, we have groups that lack any formal organization and have no capacity to coordinate their efforts, although they can share important interests. Such is the case, for instance, with the many farmers affected by drought in the developing world who may have to rely on NGOs for their representation.

All of these different kinds of groups can be represented in different ways. What we now need to examine is how.

Groups with a mind of their own

As we saw in the last chapter, the simplest model of representation follows a classic principal–agent format. In this model, one person (the principal) appoints another (the agent) to perform some action/function on his/her behalf. This presupposes that the principal has the capacity to act, since authorizing an agent is a form of action. Can certain groups be understood as principals who are capable of authorizing

Figure 4.1   The group's collective action

Inputs
The group members' individual judgements or decisions

Mechanism

Output

agents? If so, then they must be capable of carrying out actions in their own right which would include that of appointing a representative.

A group is at its most basic a set of individuals. Therefore, if a group is to have the capacity to act, this capacity must be somehow derived from the actions of its constitutive parts: i.e., individuals. This means that if the group is to act as *one* principal, there must be some mechanism whereby the *many* 'inputs' of its members (their individual judgements and/or decisions) are integrated into *one* 'output' at the group level (the group's collective decision) (see figure 4.1).

What sort of mechanism can this be? Although its specific character varies from group to group, it always takes the form of some rule, or a set of rules – whether more formal or more informal, agreed by the members of the group, or imposed from the outside – whereby the *inputs* of the group's members are put together to generate a group collective decision as their *output*.

Unanimity

The simplest example of this is a group of individuals who decide to act together on the basis of unanimous decision. Whenever all the members of a group agree on a specific course of action, the decision is simultaneously ascribable to each of the group members and to the group as a whole. One such decision can be that of authorizing an agent to act, or perform some function, on the group's behalf before a third party. So unanimous groups can readily appoint representatives.

Take, for instance, the case of a group of haemophiliacs infected with HIV by a transfusion received in an NHS hospital. They may agree to appoint the same lawyer to represent them against the hospital in a court case. This means that whenever the lawyer addresses the court, she will be speaking on behalf of a group – i.e., a number of individuals who have suffered a common injury, and whose interests she was employed to promote – while, at the same time, speaking in the name of all the members of the group. This gives them a stake in her action, which they must be able to assert in some way.

The possibility of objecting to the lawyer's action is critical because even where a group agrees unanimously to appoint a representative, they may come to disagree in their assessment of her performance. This is especially so when representation spans a lengthy period of time and the representative is given some degree of discretion. The question that arises in a democratic or non-Hobbesian setting is therefore whether a unanimously authorized representative, like a lawyer, can continue to represent the group in the face of objections of some of its members.

There seems no reason why not. Where there was no previous agreement to give each of the group members a veto power over the representative's performance, there is no need to sever the tie of representation in the face of minority objection. Any member who seriously objects to what the representative is doing in the group's name is free to express her disagreement by exiting the group, and thus opting out of the group's representation.

The group members can, however, choose to assert their stake in their agent's action in another way: through close instruction. In this case, the requirement of unanimity will most likely hamper the group's capacity to decide, or at least to take decisions within a reasonable timeframe, and lead its agent to paralysis. Unanimous decision-making is a cumbersome, inefficient and time-consuming way towards group agency and group representation. In some circumstances it may be relatively easy for a group of individuals to decide unanimously that they need a representative; but it will be much harder for them to decide unanimously what that representative should do on their behalf.

Majority

Groups may therefore decide to act together on the basis of a less burdensome rule, such as majority voting. Whatever the majority then decides is the decision of them all and obliges them all equally.

This was how various authors within the contract tradition conceptualized the foundation of the commonwealth. As we saw in chapter 1, Hobbes thought of the state as being instituted when a multitude of men *unanimously* agreed ('every one, with every one') that whatsoever (man or assembly) got the endorsement of the majority had the '*Right* to Present the Person of them all, (that is to say, to be their *Representative*;) every one, as well he that *Voted for it*, as he that *Voted against it*' (Hobbes 1996: 121).The requirement of unanimity preceding the majority decision did not mean that one person by refusing consent could stop the rest from uniting; rather, it meant that those who did not consent did not become members of the commonwealth and remained in the state of nature.

Hobbes wanted this sort of arrangement in order to rule out the possibility of any member of the group subsequently being able to object to what a representative does in the group's name. But the principle of majority voting can also be used to construct a group agent that is able to appoint a representative in ways that parallel the performance of a single individual person. This means that the group will be able to act the part of a principal, responsible for setting up a principal–agent representative relation that more closely parallels that between individuals, with the possibility of issuing instructions as well as merely subjecting themselves to representation. The voice of the majority can then be used to decide whether the group as a whole is happy with the representative's performance.

However, where representation rests on majority voting rather than unanimous decision, then some of the problems of collective action that Hobbes wanted to circumvent are bound to arise. Where majorities decide, it is inevitable that some individuals will have their objections overruled. Members of the outvoted minority, especially if they belong to a permanent minority, may want to claim that, since their views are not being represented, they are no longer obliged by the group representative's actions. This was a possibility Madison foresaw when he warned against the dangers of the 'tyranny of the majority'. In a heterogeneous group, any faction with irresistible power might take hold of representative institutions, to rule at the expense of the interests of numerical minorities, and even contrary to the 'permanent and aggregate interests of the community' as a whole (Madison et al. 2005: 48).

As Madison knew, majority rule is questionable as a principle of fairness, unless it is conducted in ways that give minorities reasons to remain attached to the political majority: namely, that losers at one time or on one issue will nevertheless have reason to think that they will be part of the winning coalition at another time or on another issue. Where such reasons are lacking, the risk of fossilized distrust is great. Different group members will also respond differently to the information and communication being fed back by representatives and third parties – any information gaps or uncertainties are likely to be greatly exacerbated in cases where certain individuals feel as though their inputs are being persistently excluded (see figure 4.2).

One way around some of these difficulties is to insist (as Hobbes did) that majority-voting procedures are underpinned by a prior unanimous decision to abide by them

Figure 4.2 Representation of majority decision (i)

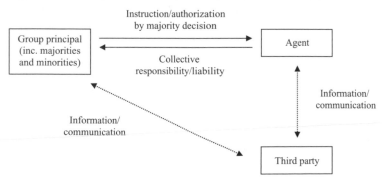

Figure 4.3   Representation of majority decision (ii)

(see figure 4.3). There are then two tiers to the representation of the group: first, the group agrees unanimously to be represented by majority decision; then the majority acts as a principal to appoint and if necessary control an agent (though Hobbes explicitly ruled out this final possibility).

But the introduction of two tiers of representation does not resolve the basic problem. Permanent minorities may plausibly insist that if the decision of the group as a whole to act by majority rule is to count as a form of representation, there must be some means for them to object to what the majority does in the group's name. Yet an arrangement of the kind described above gives them no options but either to abide by majority decision or to exit the group. Indeed, any other alternative opens up the prospect of a regress, since it is hard to see how the group as a whole can object to the decisions of its majority, unless the group appoints an alternative representative to express that dissent, a decision which will itself always be subject to majority objection. The principle of representation itself does not appear to offer protection to minorities when it comes to collective decision-making; instead, it suggests that groups that wish to be durably represented by majority decision will have to work hard to ensure that they do not contain permanent minorities.

There is a further problem with the principle of majority voting and group representation that derives from the fact that there is more than one way for a majority decision to represent the group. The problem arises when groups face decisions that require conclusions to be drawn from premise-based reasoning. Individuals may reach decisions about separate premises that lead a majority of group members to oppose a conclusion that is supported by the group as a whole, reasoning on a premise-by-premise basis. This paradox is known as 'the discursive dilemma' and can be illustrated as follows (see Kornhauser and Sager 1993). Imagine

Table 4.1 Collective decision (i)

	Harm? (P)	Duty of Care? (Q)	Liable (P&Q)
A	Yes	No	No
B	Yes	Yes	Yes
C	No	Yes	No
Majority vote	Yes	Yes	NO

a three-member jury (A, B and C) who must establish a majority view on whether someone is guilty of a tort. To that end, they must determine whether that person did harm (P), had a duty of care (Q) and therefore would be liable for damages (P&Q). Their votes are shown in table 4.1.

Although the individual votes of the jurors are entirely consistent, the majority verdict, which results from the aggregation of votes with respect to the conclusion (the liability issue) is self-contradictory: that (P), that (Q), and that not (P&Q). This shows that when we decide to maximize responsiveness to the views of a group's members, by taking decisions on the basis of majority vote on its members' conclusions, we run into collective inconsistency.

One way around this difficulty is to accept that the group decision may trump the majority choices of individual members. This is known as the process of 'collectivizing reason' (Pettit 2003). It is achieved by making the group's decision follow from majority approval of separate premises, rather than from the majority preferences of separate individuals. The result is that the group may collectively reach a decision that a majority of its members individually reject, even though the group's decision still results from member preferences, tabulated on a premise-by-premise basis. Table 4.2 illustrates this, using the previous example.

The group's decision ('Yes') is, as we can see, discontinuous with that of its members (the majority of whom say 'No'). When acting on this basis, the group is therefore acting as an intentional subject, with a mind of its own, that is independent of the views of its individual members. That is, the group

Table 4.2   Collective decision (ii)

	Harm? (P)	Duty of Care? (Q)	Liable? (P&Q)
A	Yes	No	No
B	Yes	Yes	Yes
C	No	Yes	No
Majority vote	Yes	Yes	YES

is acting as a subject in its own right. There is no reason why such a subject should not also be able to act as a principal in order to appoint a representative and also to issue that representative with instructions (in this case, assuming the jury has a spokesperson, the instruction would be to announce the liability of the defendant).

But what we notice here is that the ability of the group to act as a principal in its own right tends to break rather than to reinforce the ties of representation between the individual and the group. Groups that have a mind of their own, in the sense of acting on the basis of collectivized reason, cannot plausibly be understood to *represent* their individual members. This is because, although the group decision is made up from the choices of individuals, the individuals themselves are not present in this decision (or at least, only a minority are). As a result, there exists a gap between two different aspects of group representation, corresponding to the two tiers described above. Groups with a mind of their own are better able to act as principals, and therefore to be represented in their own right; but such groups are less well able to act as the representatives of their individual members and bind them to group decisions. The discursive dilemma highlights an enduring tension in the idea of group representation: the stronger a group's capacity to be represented in its own right, the weaker may be its capacity to represent its individual members.

This has a number of wider implications. One concerns the question of collective responsibility. As we saw in the previous chapter, principal–agent relationships understood in the terms of representation often imply certain responsibilities on the part of principals for the actions of their agents. But in the case of group principals, those responsibilities may also have to be distributed among the groups members. The more 'collectivized' the group – in the sense of the group having an identity over and above that of its individual members – the less the scope for strict forms of collective responsibility. This in turn places a great premium – for groups that wish to collectivize their decision-making procedures but also to represent their individual members in a way that permits the collective distribution of responsibilities – on the prior consent of members to be bound in this way. Pettit suggests that groups which collectivize reason must allow individual members to decide on a case-by-case basis whether they wish to be represented by the collective decisions of the group. So we are back with unanimity and exit as the grounds for non-unanimous collective decision-making, with all the restrictions that this entails.

What is clear is that the scope for groups to act on both sides of the principal–agent relationship – that is, both as principals capable of being represented and as agents capable of representing the members of the group – is extremely narrow. Such groups will need to be sure of the consent of individual members to their procedures, to allow individuals a way out (or at least a means of expressing their dissent) when they find themselves on the wrong end of group decisions, and perhaps even to appoint what Pettit calls 'plenipotentiaries' to assist individuals in the business of coordinating their views. There are some groups that potentially fit this description: small-scale workers' cooperatives are one; a judicial bench like the United States Supreme Court is another. But there are many groups that do not fit, either because they lack the capacity for collectivized reason or because they lack the relevant safeguards for individual members. One obvious such group is the nation-state. States are too diverse and disaggregated for collectivised reason; moreover, they invariably lack suitably robust exit mechanisms. As a result, the representation of a group like the state cannot be satisfactorily accounted for in a principal–agent model of this kind.

However, the major limitation of this model as a generalized account of representation is that it presupposes that the group has some capacity to act prior to the action of its representative. It is this presupposition that makes this model distinctively anti-Hobbesian and readily illustrates the ways in which Hobbes neglected the possibility of other forms of group representation than his preferred model of collective authorization. But Hobbes was right that some groups, including but by no means limited to the state, may not be able act on their own and may find themselves dependent on a representative for their capacity for collective decision-making. For these groups it may well turn out that a plenipotentiary has not merely to coordinate group decisions but also to take decisions on behalf of the group as well. This is a possibility that cannot be accommodated by conceptions of representation that presuppose a group principal with a mind of its own. To make sense of the representation of groups that cannot act in their own right, and to see how it might still be possible to get beyond a reductively Hobbesian world-view, we need to turn to the second model of representation: trusteeship.

Trusts and corporations

There are many groups in our society that cannot act except through a representative, either because they are too big, too dispersed, or lack mechanisms of coordination among all their members. Where groups are incapable of acting in their own right, they cannot authorize, much less instruct, a representative to perform actions on their behalf. The representative must therefore receive its power from a source other than the group itself. But what source can this be? For Hobbes, it could only be the sovereign state. But can we find any other way of holding an arrangement of this kind together?

Looking at the legal model of a 'trust' can give us an idea of how such schemes do actually work in practice before we consider what their wider application might be. Beginning with the legal concept of trusteeship as a template for other kinds of collective representation is a common strategy in various forms of political thought. Locke, for instance, believed the people could act as a community, setting limits on government by means of relations of trust, and he employed the notion of 'tacit trust' to stress the fiduciary nature of all political power. The legal concept of trust was used by Locke to stress the ruler's responsibility to serve the public good but also to highlight the asymmetry of power which makes it hard for the ruled to exercise any continuing effective control over their representatives (Dunn 1984).

But what is the underlying basis of the idea of a legal trust that allows it to be deployed in this way? In common law, a trust is an arrangement whereby money or property is managed by one person (or persons, or organization) – the trustee – for the benefit of another person (or persons, or organization), without the beneficiaries being said to own the property in question. A concrete example may help to clarify how this works.

The mining industrialist, Mr B., is committed to improving the standard of living for his workers. Given the health risks involved in mining, he establishes a charitable trust to provide financial help for former employees suffering hardship due to illness. For that purpose, he appoints a group of trustees who are responsible for holding and administering the assets of the trust for the employees' benefit (see figure 4.4).

Figure 4.4 Model of a charitable trust

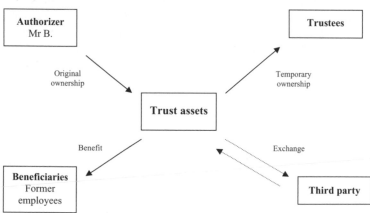

There are two main things to notice here.

- First: the *unspecified* nature of the group of beneficiaries of the trust, which in itself accounts for their incapacity to act as a group in their own right. The potential group of beneficiaries comprises all the past and future employees subject to work-related illnesses. This means that there is never a moment in time when the whole group of beneficiaries is simultaneously 'present' and capable of asserting its own interests. There are always the interests of future generations of workers to be accounted for. This can be done only through this form of representation.
- Second: the new and more intricate chain of responsibility. The trustees must hold and invest the assets of the trust for the benefit of its group of beneficiaries. Whatever they do with those assets will inevitably have consequences for the beneficiaries' well-being. However, the trustees are not bound by the wishes of the beneficiaries in their managerial decisions. (Nor could they be, since, as we have seen, this group lacks agency and is incapable of having 'wishes' as such.) They are rather bound by the expectations of the originator of the trust, without being his representatives.

Charitable trusts provide us with an insight into the parties that may be involved in the representation of groups who cannot act for themselves. But, as a general model, they must be treated with caution. Strictly speaking, they are not cases of representation. Trustees act neither in the name of the trust settler, nor of the trust beneficiaries: they are their own persons. Second, trusts are deeply legal creations. They rely on property rights, and the legal framework that established such rights, as the basis for their construction; and they rely on the courts for their enforcement.

Nevertheless, everywhere we look in our societies, we see groups of individuals that are incapable of acting on their own but which have nevertheless acquired a separate personal identity by being represented *as though* they possessed such an identity and could act in the manner of principals. This is achieved by having representatives acting in the group's name and on its behalf, in accordance with rules that treat the group as if it were a single principal. That is, a multitude of individuals can incorporate themselves into an artificial principal by following rules of representation, establishing who can act on the group's behalf and holding the group, as a separate entity, responsible for those actions. This is the point at which the idea of trusteeship moves towards the model of the corporation.

We saw an early version of this model at work in arguments of the medieval period surrounding the political identity of associations such as communes and city-states that wished to be treated as corporate entities. In modern legal discourse, as an artificial person created by law, the corporation has a personality that is separate and distinct from its owners – for example, the group of shareholders who hold the common stock – and it enjoys most of the rights and responsibilities that are normally possessed by principals: entering into contracts, lending and borrowing money, suing and being sued, and so on. The truth however is that corporations cannot act on their own. All their activities are carried out by different representatives acting for them, in their stead. These are known as the corporation's officers. Only they can bind the corporation to contracts and agreements with third parties.

Let us imagine, for instance, that the corporation hires a corporate lawyer. Because the corporation is an artificial principal, the lawyer's client is the corporation itself, not its management. If he or she enters a legal action on the company's behalf, and loses the case, who is to bear the ultimate consequences? The answer is the corporation itself, since the liability of the individual shareholders is limited. That, in fact, is frequently the purpose of incorporation: to ensure that individual members are not each personally responsible for what is done in the group's name. Here again is an instance where the more distinct the identity of a group, the easier it is to separate out the group's responsibilities from those of its individual members for actions carried out on the group's behalf.

The rules of representation, authorization and accountability are potentially highly complex in this model (see figure 4.5). The lawyer acts on the authority of the body of directors. The directors have received their power to act, and to authorize others to act on the corporation's behalf, from the shareholders, the company's owners. Directors are bound by

Figure 4.5 Representation as incorporation

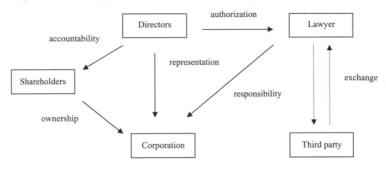

the expectations of the shareholders but they do not simply represent individual shareholders and their interests. They also represent the corporation as a whole and have the fiduciary duty to act for the benefit of the corporation itself. This means that (1) they are free to do for the corporation what is best in their judgement and (2) that the corporation is accountable for the consequences of their actions and of the actions of inferior officers, whenever carried out within the limits of their representative mandate.

But representative actions might not always be carried out in the corporation's best interest. When this is the case, the corporation, being an incapable entity, cannot object to how it is being represented. But someone must be able to do so, if the corporation's interests are not merely being looked after but rather being *represented*. For example, the shareholders can assert a competing claim to speak on the corporation's behalf. When sufficient numbers of shareholders object to the directors' representation of the corporation's interests, they can cut the tie of representation, either by not re-electing the directors and removing them from office, or by taking them to court for violation of the duty of care. The question of whether their objections are decisive, or not, is then decided by an impartial arbitrator: the judge.

As this example shows, groups can be represented as having identities, and interests, of their own which are separate from those of their individual members; moreover, this can be done without recourse to the devices of collectivized reason. But the problem with this otherwise attractive model of group representation is that the rules of representation that allow the group to act as an artificial principal have to be external to the group, since the group cannot act without its representative. This is precisely because the group does *not* have a mind of its own. Even the decision to establish the group cannot be the decision *of* the group because the group established through incorporation is distinct from the individuals to whom it belongs. Incorporation is not merely a means of organization, it is also a mode of transformation and depends on outside help. This dependency on external agency explains the legalistic nature of the examples that have been so far given. It also explains why this formal legal model, for all its complexity and flexibility, may be of limited help when trying to think about politics. Some corporate bodies, such as states themselves, operate in less legally controlled environments. How might they be represented on this account?

To consider this possibility, we need to focus on the representative's obligation to further the group's *interests*. A representative must make the group's interests *present* when he or she deals with third parties on the group's behalf. But these interests do not need to constitute an objective category, established prior to representation. Indeed they hardly ever do. They are rather established within the process of representation itself.

This means that representation does not require that the group has formulated a clear sense of its own interests before the representative acts on its behalf. Certainly the group cannot will its own interest independently of its representative. Groups that are incapable entities cannot form such a will prior to their being represented but they can be represented as though they possessed such a will. Indeed, they rely on their representatives for precisely that function: they must *interpret* the group's interest, and in so doing put forth a claim to be representing it. This claim, by its very interpretative nature, is open to be challenged by rival claims of different representatives who can give the group's interests a separate (and, they think, more satisfactory) presence. If competing claims arise, a representative must be able to offer plausible reasons for what he or she is doing on the group's behalf. This explains the centrality of the notion of account-ability to this broader model of group representation. This is not accountability through group sanction, as the group cannot act against the representative in its own right, but accountability in the sense of being able to give public accounts, and provide good reasons, for the legitimacy of any self-standing claim to representation.

In the absence of strict legal rules, all forms of corporate representation are liable to be subject to competing claims to speak in the name of the group. This competition between rival representatives is a distinctive feature of any form of representation of groups understood as extra-legal corporate entities. Because the group cannot speak for itself, but given representation requires that there should be some means of objecting to what is said on the group's behalf, all objections will have to come in the form of alternative acts of represen-tation. As we shall see in the next chapter, this feature of group representation has profound implications for the politi-cal representation of collectives on the scale of modern states, which will always be subject to such competing claims. Com-petition for the claim to speak authoritatively on behalf of the group can help in assessing the credentials of rival repre-sentatives but it cannot settle them once and for all. In this sense, the representation of such groups is always an ongoing process.

The other feature that is distinctive of corporate models of group representation, and which they share in common with trustee models, is their emphasis on the ascription of rights and responsibilities. This is what ties these models to their legal origins. Representation on these accounts is primarily understood as a means of deciding what belongs to whom and who must take responsibility for what. Crucial to these models, therefore, is the business of authorization, by which various rights and responsibilities are transferred between parties. In the case of corporate representation, a group person is specifically created with the purpose of being the bearer of such rights and responsibilities – in the words of the legal historian F. W. Maitland, a corporation is simply a 'rights-and-duties-bearing-unit' and, as Maitland recog-nized, this is as true of the state as of any other corporate body (Maitland 2003). However, it is not true of all groups, and this focus on authorization and transfer does not hold for all models of group representation. There is another, very different way of thinking about what it means to be the representative of a group's interests: this occurs when individuals represent groups not on the basis of their having been authorized to do so but simply because these are groups to which, in some sense, they belong.

Interests and identities

Group representation need not presuppose the appointment of a representative who agrees to act on the group's behalf. A group's representative can be self-selected. She can bring forward a claim to represent the group, which is proved retrospectively by her capacity to attract a following: i.e., a group of people who see themselves as having a presence in her actions. But it can also be the other way round. A group can make someone into their representative, irrespective of her will, because they identify with something she does, or something she stands for.

Both of these possibilities are present wherever groups are sets of 'like-minded' individuals, who can be represented simply by dint of what they have in common. These commonalities may give a group of individuals a presence in the actions of another person. They can vary from interests and descriptive characteristics to social perspectives, values and insights. They may also overlap with other forms of representation in which legal or semi-legal modes of authorization play a part. But representation as identification, as opposed to representation by means of incorporation, does not depend on either authority or accountability claims in order to function.

Interest groups

Interests are the most common things that individuals are likely to share. People who, for instance, have the same risky profession, say firefighters, are likely to have a common interest in security measures that can reduce risk. So if someone mounts a public campaign, in an attempt to get funding for the acquisition of adequate personal protective equipment, she will be seen as acting for the group as a whole. This is not solely because she is acting in the group's interests – she could after all be acting in their interests by financing the campaign without representing them. It is rather because (1) she is making their interests *present* in her interaction with third parties (e.g., the general public, government, corporations, etc.); and (2) firefighter associations can assert their *presence* by objecting to her campaign. Defending interests, without this capacity for asserting presence, does not make for a case of representation. But where this capacity exists, in the absence of a clear legal framework, there also exists the possibility of ongoing contestation. Hence interest group representation of this kind is inherently political.

The reason why interests are such a contested category is that they are never totally objective. They are not simply things objectively at stake, or mere 'givens' waiting to be advanced through representation. On the contrary, they require articulation, aggregation, hierarchical ordering. Group interests will be constructed in the process of representation itself. They are more objective than, say, wishes, in that wishes must always be someone's and interests can potentially be detached from any specific group of 'holders' (for example, a collective interest in peace or in a sustainable environment can be cross-cutting, in a way that makes it no one's and everyone's). But interests are never totally unattached either: if the advancement of certain interests proves to be of no interest to anyone, then no claim to group representation on this basis is likely to be sustainable. This dualistic character of interests, both attached and unattached, subjective and objective, lies at the heart of the ambiguities inherent in any form of interest group representation (Pitkin 1967).

Of course, many interest groups will also fall into the category of group principals or corporate agents. But the representation of groups of individuals on account of shared interests rests on a wider base than the representation of the groups we have discussed so far in this chapter. This is for two main reasons.

- First, interest groups do not necessarily have agreed procedures of decision-making (as will be the case with an ad hoc protest coalition), nor do they need to have formal identities, although some of them will (as with lobbyists on behalf of certain interests, like the NRA in the United States).
- Second, interest representation can and often does cut across actual group membership. People can be represented because of interests they have in common, despite the fact that they belong to different groups. For instance, a coalition of protesters against airport expansion, whose spokesperson takes part in a TV debate, may include groups as varied as angry local residents, environmental scientists, supporters of the anti-capitalist movement, environmental associations, political parties and farmers' associations, all of them fighting for a common cause, albeit for different reasons (quality of life, property value, climate change, etc).

As a result, interest group representation can take various different forms and involve many different models of representation. These often have echoes of more legalistic forms of representation but cannot simply be reduced to them. Nor can they be divorced from the political context in which they occur. Interest group representation always depends on which interests people think are worth fighting for and defending.

One possible way of capturing this is through the model of *functional representation*. This model is historically associated with the doctrine of political pluralism and, in particular, with the pluralist claim that individuals ought to be represented according to *what they actually do*, rather than where they happen to live, or the formal political organizations to which they belong, because it is what they do that matters.

Samuel Beer defined functional representation as referring to 'any theory that finds the community divided into various *strata*, regards each of these *strata* as having a certain corporate unity, and holds that they ought to be represented in government' (Beer 1965: 71). This idea had an especial currency in the first decades of the twentieth century. The

interests thought to deserve representation were then generally regarded as those arising from the division of labour,
and the relevant *strata* as being economic groupings such
as employers, labour and farmers. Across Europe, various
assemblies emerged where functional interests of a commercial, industrial and agrarian nature were given direct representation. In most cases, in an echo of the medieval notions
from which this model derives, they fulfilled purposes of both
representation *and* control: i.e., they secured state control
over their respective areas of economic life and compliance
with agreed state policy.

But the functional model of interest representation suffered
from a lack of conceptual distinctiveness. It did not explain
how representatives were to be answerable to the functional
groups they represented, unless they were to be answerable
to them in the more conventional ways, such as election,
instruction, incorporation, and so on. Of course, there is no
reason why functional groups such as trade unions should
not adopt conventional models of representation. But the
problem is that functional representation seems to promise
more than this – indeed, the central part of its appeal has
always been that it offers a means to go beyond the constraints and limitations that conventional groups impose on
their members. Yet it can only do this in so far as it is something other than a model of group representation; in so far
as it is a form of representation, political pluralism is subject
to the limitations of the other models.

The views of the English pluralist G. D. H. Cole (1889–
1959), the leading champion of guild socialism, epitomize
this conceptual deadlock. He maintained, in classic Rousseauan fashion, that no man can represent another, 'because
no man's will can be treated as a substitute for, or representative of, the wills of others' (Cole 1920: 103). But to this he
added that the common goals of an association of men could
be represented because every association 'has a specific object
or objects' which its members have previously determined as
desirable. To represent an association was tantamount to
furthering its objects, or the group's predetermined interests.
Functional interest representation was therefore moulded
upon a classic principal–agent format: the representative (or
as guild socialists sometimes put it, the 'mandated delegate')

promises to follow the group's express interests. Guild social-ism thus sought to combine two familiar but not easily rec-oncilable positions: one that opposes the representation of individuals *qua* individuals and the other that champions the representation of groups in their own right. To hold both positions requires an account of how groups can have a mind of their own independently of the minds of the individuals who happen to be their members. The political pluralists, despite their best efforts, never came up with a satisfactory account of how groups could act in their own right and some of them ended up flirting with corporatist or even proto-fascist conceptions of group personality, of a kind that ulti-mately subsumed the individual within the group (Runciman 1997). In this respect, early twentieth-century theories of functional representation rested on a certain amount of wishful thinking.

Despite its indistinctiveness as a model of representation, and the relatively short shelf-life of this brand of political pluralism as a political movement (it was effectively finished by the 1930s), functional representation has survived into the twenty-first century. In many ways it is more prevalent today than it was ever before. But this means we had to move from the *direct* functional representation of economic interests, understood as a form of corporatism, to the *indirect* func-tional representation of interests in competing lobbying schemes. As a result, functional representation now deals with a much expanded sense of those areas in which individu-als can see their interests being advanced or thwarted: not only the economic, but also the social, the environmental, or indeed the political.

But if the interests requiring representation have multiplied, the central idea of functional representation remains unal-tered: that is, that we should not let any single representative stand for us in all our interests but rather have different rep-resentatives for the different interests we might have. This explains why the model of functional interest-group represen-tation concentrates not so much on representation as a group experience as on whether the significant interests present in a society, at any one given time, are being represented within the system as a whole. If they are, they are also expected to police and check one another, in order to ensure that individuals do not end up being dominated by particular groupings at the expense of others. In the next two chapters we will consider whether this offers a plausible model of political representation at, or even beyond, the level of the state.

Functional representation presupposes a relative durability in the interests shared between individuals, allowing a system of representation to establish itself over time. Other interest groups, however, are not only much more informal but also relatively short-lived. They are spontaneous collusions of people sharing a common concern over a particular, time-bound issue. Such is the case with many forms of political protest that are quick to arise in response to some crisis or outrage, display strong indications of short-term group identification but in the absence of the initial motivation or cause are quick to dissipate. This has been the story of many modern anti-war movements, from Vietnam in the late 1960s and early 1970s through to Iraq in 2003. The tendency of these movements, after the initial rush of enthusiasm, is to devolve into a narrower, more committed group of protestors, whose preoccupation with the subject makes it harder for them to represent the more diverse and less focused concerns of the general public. However, other interest groups survive, and even prosper, on the basis of this sort of discrepancy between the core activists and a less focused and broader coalition of sympathizers. This is true of a wide range of causes, from anti-abortion to environmentalism. Indeed, it could be argued that much contemporary 'issue-based' politics revolves around the willingness of small groups of individuals to act on behalf of larger groups with whom they share a set of concerns but from whom they are divided by their far greater willingness to get involved (Stoker 2006).

This raises some important questions for the theory of representation which the models of group representation we have discussed so far do not address. What is the basis of the claim of activists to represent those whose concerns are much more passive? It cannot be formal structures of authorization or incorporation because in such cases there aren't any. But nor can it be straightforward notions of identification, because the sympathizers do not identify with the activists in the sense that they might behave similarly in a similar situation. The salient fact about the passivity of most people in the face of the issues that concern them is that they have deliberately chosen to behave in ways that do not fully commit them to the cause. Nor is it enough to say that what is being shared here between the representatives and the wider group are common interests, since the levels of interest so clearly differ between different individuals. Instead, there is at best a loose identification around a set of hopes for the future and perhaps a shared set of emotional responses. Whether or not this is sufficient to generate a sustainable form of politics, it is clear that as a model of representation, in which one group of people is given presence in the actions of another, it is far weaker than other competing models, in which the ties between representative and represented are much more clearly defined.

If anything, the variety of these examples proves that there are not one but many types of interest-group representation. The common denominator is that in all of them the represented and the representative are connected by means of interests they share. But the details vary widely. At times, interest groups bring with them the authorization and accountability mechanisms of voluntary associations (i.e., clearly defined membership criteria, internal mechanisms for dissent and opportunities for exit). At other times, they rely on self-appointed representatives and on the competition between different such representatives to stand in for those more formal mechanisms of accountability and authorization. Or they can rest on even more ad hoc processes of identification and sympathy, which may be unable to survive even the slightest competition from better established groups.

This highlights another significant feature of this form of representation: there will not just be competition between individuals to represent the group; there will also be competition between different groups to represent separate individuals with all their various interests. Prioritizing variety over uniformity, by providing different representatives for the different interests that people have, may well provide an extra reassurance that group interests are being acted on and their presence asserted in the actions of our political representatives. This is the lingering hope of functional representation. But the automatic benefits expected from this variety encounter two difficulties: (1) What are we to do in the face of serious conflicts arising between representatives representing the same individuals in different capacities (e.g., as citizens and as consumers)? And (2) what about the necessity to create outlets for those individuals' objections to the system of representation as a whole? Variety can be gained at the cost of incoherence and can so gridlock political processes that no single entity can take responsibility for the advancement of the interests of the public as a whole. This is one of the themes of the next chapter.

Identity groups

Besides particular interests, people can also be represented on account of a more basic identity they share: that is, on account of what they perceive themselves, and are perceived by others, to be. As Charles Taylor has stressed, different groups of individuals are vulnerable to the ways in which they are perceived by others, especially where this reflects back to them a demeaning image of themselves (Taylor 1994). This reflected image can lead people to identify around a common experience of discrimination or social stigma, which is attached to characteristics they share, and has become central – often negatively central – to their identities. Some of these characteristics may be things we come to share accidentally. This is readily exemplified by people who have the same infectious and potentially stigmatizing disease, such as HIV/AIDS or leprosy. Of course, such people will have interests in common. But they may also find themselves being represented by individuals with whom they simply happen to share certain salient characteristics.

This is the literal extension of the idea of the 'poster child' discussed in the previous chapter. In the case of a child afflicted by a disease or a deformity whose picture is used on posters to raise money for charitable purposes, the representation is mere symbolism, rather than a form of agency. But the term is now used more widely, meaning someone who typifies a group of persons and as such is able to speak or act on their behalf. Such is the case, for instance, with individuals who, having been subject to discrimination on the basis of characteristics they share with others (e.g., being HIV-positive), make the headlines, acting as spokespersons for the group's grievances. Their representative status springs from their speaking for the group authoritatively, with the voice of experience.

This was, for instance, the case with Ryan White, an otherwise inconspicuous teenager from Indiana, who became the North American poster child for AIDS-related prejudice during the 1980s and early 1990s. His case caught the public eye when he was evicted from the public school he attended and his family filed a lawsuit seeking to overturn the ban. As the case received media attention, as well as support from various public figures, White became the face of those suffering from similar discrimination and was expected to speak on their behalf. As often happens in cases of identity representation, White had not consented to become a spokesperson. But he became one anyway. Identity representation does without formal mechanisms of authorization to representation and even of the representative's acceptance of his or her new representative status.

This form of representation puts us in the domain of *ascriptive* identity groups. For groups of individuals can be represented on the basis of ascriptive identifications, resulting from their common membership in the same involuntary group. These identifications are called 'ascriptive', in the sense of being beyond the person's immediate control. They are determined by categories into which we are born, not ones we choose or can change easily – such as country, family, caste, religion, race, ethnicity or gender (as opposed to more changeable identity criteria, such as political ideology).

The assumption behind the use of descriptive representatives – that is, representatives who bear the defining attributes of an ascriptive group – is that some sense of the predictability of their behaviour is given by their possession of the relevant attributes. These are taken as external indicators of the likelihood of the representative acting as the group members would in the face of similar circumstances. Representation by someone who is 'one of us' therefore works as a kind of cognitive division of labour. Given that sensible people have better things to do than to work out, all by themselves, every single policy, or piece of legislation, they entrust someone who is sufficiently 'like them' with the task of picking the policies, and passing the legislation, they themselves would have adopted if they had all the relevant information and the time to process it.

John Stuart Mill touched upon this idea when he voiced his concerns about the proper representation of the labouring class: 'Does Parliament, or almost any of the members composing it,' Mill asked, 'ever for an instant look at any question with the eyes of a working man?' (Mill 1991: 246). Workers needed sympathetic representatives, capable of interpreting the public interest from *their* point of view. Mill was writing at a time when social class, as defined by work, figured chiefly amongst people's identifications. But at least since the 1960s, class has been losing some of its political visibility and identities other than class, or political ideology, have come to bear greater significance (e.g., ethnicity, race, gender, etc.). The relative weight of our various identifications has thus been changing but the expectation that representatives who are *like us* will act as we would remains broadly unchanged.

How reasonable is this expectation? On some accounts, it seems wholly unreasonable, if it is premised on unwarranted essentialist conceptions of identity. These posit one aspect of identity (say, 'woman-ness') as automatically determining the group members' experiences, views and behaviour in respect to most issues. However, the truth is that the social meaning attached to any particular woman's identity might be so different as to render the project of representing one woman in terms of what she shares with other women virtually meaningless. Even women living in close proximity – such as a Brazilian black maid and her white employer – might live worlds apart. Women like these may experience the category of 'gender' and the social meanings attached to it in such different ways that we would look in vain for an 'authentic' woman's experience. Essentialist views of identity are dangerously misleading in that they result in a denial of the instability and internal heterogeneity of identity categories. They collide with the idea that a plurality of perspectives may co-exist, and potentially conflict, in any given identity group, or even in any given individual.

This raises a difficulty which is intimately tied to the problem of representation – if no one woman can know the experiences of all women, on what authority can she ever speak 'as a woman': i.e., accurately speak for and about women at all? Can identities be non-essential, and yet epistemically and politically significant, so that our trust in representatives who are *like* us might amount to more than a mere leap of faith? It seems it can, if we take into consideration a further, less contentious claim: goods, opportunities and resources are still, in many societies, distributed according to identity categories, making identity a key element of social oppression, as well as social liberation. This is because: (1) ascriptive attributes are often the basis for negative stereotyping of certain group identities; (2) ascriptive attributes are often used to assign positions of worth in society, in ways that affect the group members' status and life chances with reference to the members of other groups, generating structural relations of power and inequalities that are clearly correlated with categories of identity; (3) these power relations work themselves upon the life histories of the group members and are likely to give rise to certain common experiences (of racial, sexual, economic discrimination, etc.), as well as to generate shared views on aspects of social reality.

These facts about group identity generate defences of representation as descriptive identification under four different rubrics:

- *Symbolism* – descriptive representatives work as role models, showing the members of chronically underrepresented groups that they are equally fit to rule, and facilitating their participation (Guinier 1994).
- *Trust* – given the record of discrimination, group members might find it easier to forge bonds of trust and communication with representatives who share with them the experience of systemic disadvantage (Mansbridge 1999).
- *Overlooked interests* – descriptive representatives, because they speak with the 'authority' of shared experience, may prove more successful in getting onto the political agenda the silenced group's concerns, interests and perspectives, raising questions about the purported impartiality of the

policy preferences of the dominant group (Williams 1998; Phillips 1998).

*   *Revitalized democracy* – when given a role in government, members of formerly disempowered groups have more reason to remain attached to, and recognize the legitimacy of, political institutions (Mansbridge 1999).

Any commitment of this kind to preserving the allegiance of all sectors of society, including traditionally underrepresented groups, is normally met with institutional remedies designed to allow disempowered groups their 'turn'. Reserved seats, party quotas, racial districting, or simply a proportional electoral system, particularly one with low thresholds, may all be used to facilitate the election of identity-based representatives. The more fluid and competitive the institutional forms of descriptive group representation, the less 'essentializing' they will also tend to be (Mansbridge 1999).

But if a shared experience of marginalization increases the likelihood that representation as descriptive identification converts into representation of the group's interests, it by no means makes it certain. It does not follow from the empirical evidence that a marginalized woman, simply because she is a woman, is the best representative for marginalized women's interests more generally. This would require not only that all such women share broadly similar interests but also that only such women are capable of representing those interests. The first of these assumptions is questionable, as we have seen, given the diversity of interests among any group of individuals; the second is equally hard to justify. People can identify with, or even experience themselves as, members of a social group with which they do not share group-defining attributes. They can do this by means of sympathy or other forms of emotional or intellectual connection. Moreover, when groups are seriously disadvantaged, limiting interest representation to those who share the relevant attributes of group membership can severely constrain the possibilities of representation altogether. As we shall see in chapter 6, some of the world's most disadvantaged people find it very hard to be heard when they speak for themselves. In such circumstances, taking the interests of the group seriously may require allowing more privileged outsiders to represent them.

It follows that identity representation and interest representation may overlap but that it would be a mistake to assume that they *must* overlap. But is there anything else that can justify representation in these terms apart from interests? One alternative is to consider identity representation through the language of shared social perspectives (Williams 1998; Phillips 1998; Young 2000). Perspectives are a looser and more flexible category than interests in that they imply an overlapping set of concerns and experiences but not necessarily a common set of objectives. It is possible to share a perspective with another person without necessarily wishing for the same outcome in any given scenario. Perhaps more importantly, representing the group in terms of its perspectives rather than simply its interests also allows the representative a greater flexibility to adjust her position in the face of discussion or deliberation. Interests are inflexible in the sense that they do not change simply by being exposed to alternative points of view; but perspectives might change in precisely this way. Representation based on identification assumes that the representative will behave as any group member might behave in similar circumstances. This, though, can make the behaviour of the group seem somewhat static, if identity representation is understood simply as a limitation on the options available, as in the idea that a woman would not do anything that would not occur to other women. But it is also possible to identify with someone who changes their mind – we might conclude that in sharing a similar perspective with our representatives, we too would shift our position if we found ourselves exposed to the same arguments.

For the champions of deliberative forms of decision-making, the representation of perspectives has the advantage over the representation of interests in that it places a premium on the ability of representatives to think for themselves while still being able to replicate the thought-processes and ideas that they might share with the people they represent. The proportional representation of interest groups in a parliamentary setting is often associated with inflexibility on the part of the representatives, as they stick to the position they feel that their 'constituency' would expect of them. The representation of perspectives, by contrast, is closer to Mill's conception of a 'congress of opinion'. But once the language of representation has been recast in terms of perspectives or opinions, it is again an open question whether ascriptive identity is the best way of deciding who should represent whom. This kind of identity may of course help – shared experiences are not easily understood by those who do not share them. But if the priority is to ensure a combination of empathy plus openness on the part of a representative, then it may be better to conceive of representation in somewhat different terms.

For example, Nadia Urbinati, drawing heavily on the work of Mill, has recently argued in favour of a conception of representation as 'advocacy', which combines 'the representative's passionate link to the cause' with 'the representative's relative autonomy of judgement' (Urbinati 2000: 773). This passionate link might be forged in the empathy of shared experience; but it might equally be the result of a deep imaginative sympathy on the part of the representative. What is needed from a good advocate is not 'existential identification' but 'an identity of ideals and projects' and the capacity to pursue them (ibid.: 777). The fact is that 'advocacy', which is at root a legal concept, places a premium on skill in argument, in order to present the cause in a way that allows others to respond to it. The question of who will make the best advocate is not always to be resolved by asking who has the most in common with the cause in question. Descriptive forms of representation are often a necessary counterpoint to other kinds of representation, particularly in a system that displays a persistent bias against the representation of certain disadvantaged groups. But they are rarely sufficient to determine who will make the best representative for any of the groups concerned.

Territorial group representation

At this point, it should be clear that questions of group representation are inextricably tied up with a set of normative political considerations. What do we want from our representatives? How do we wish them to relate to each other? In what setting should these interactions take place? These questions are in turn linked to a number of the questions that came out of the historical story we told in the first part of this book. What sort of representation is on offer within the setting of the state? How can the state itself be represented? Should the state still be understood as the primary locus of political representation? These are the questions that will be discussed in the final part of this book.

But before we do, it is important to make one final observation about group representation. In almost all polities, the dominant form of group representation is territorial. The basic fact of modern politics is that almost everywhere citizens are represented by where they happen to live, whether this location is a municipality, a province, a county, a district or a state. Territorial constituencies are such a prominent feature of our political landscape that it often seems natural for political representation to be determined by geography. But as with any kind of representation, there is little that is natural about it. Representation by constituency is only one among a range of possible ways of connecting individuals up into groups; and there are a number of different ways in which the representation of groups of this kind can be conceived. Accordingly, territorial representation does not automatically fit any of the models of group representation we have previously analysed but it is capable of displaying elements of them all.

Territorial constituencies are frequently justified on the grounds that they allow for the representation of local 'communities of interest'. Given that territory often captures relevant socio-economic interests (e.g., rural vs. urban), this can be a means of giving these interests separate representation at the national level. They can then be balanced against one another in the formulation of public policy, and in the allocation of territorially specific goods, such as highways, schools or hospitals. The problem with depicting territorial representation as a case of interest group representation, however, is that the modern territorial constituency is often too large or fluid to represent any 'community of interest' coherently, and the old territorial divisions (including rural vs. urban) are frequently less salient than they once were (certain cultural issues, such as fox-hunting in Great Britain, notwithstanding).

There is also the question of deciding how such groups should best be represented. The places where people live often define who they are, even when they do not share common interests with other individuals in the same geographical area. Territorial divides like North/South, rural/urban, or coastal/inland are therefore presented as being conterminous not only with different communities of interest but also with different cultural identities and community perspectives. Local representatives may be best equipped to represent these perspectives, in so far as they are 'one of them', and share their defining experiences (for instance, their 'rural-ness', their 'northern-ness', their sense of isolation, caused by their distance from centres of decision-making, and so on). However, given current patterns of geographical mobility, and the internal diversity of modern constituencies, this argument also looks tenuous: it is increasingly hard to see identity communities as geographically localized, certainly within traditional constituency boundaries. Indeed, as we will discuss in the next chapter, getting constituency boundaries to match the domain of group identity usually requires the aid of gerrymandering, with counter-productive results.

An alternative, then, is to look away from shared local interests or shared identities and to focus instead on the ways in which constituencies may be seen as principals, able to direct the actions of their representatives in some contexts and, at the very least, to assert their agency in the act of selecting those representatives. Constituency control can take two main forms. Constituents can choose a representative who shares their views, so that in following her convictions she realizes their policy preferences. Or the representative follows her perception of her constituency's preferences because she seeks to win re-election. However, here again we run up against the persistent difficulty that geographical constituencies will invariably be too large, poorly integrated and diverse for this to be achieved with any great efficiency. And traditional constituencies certainly lack the cooperative mechanisms required for any form of collectivized reason.

Underlying the difficulty of fitting territorial representation neatly into any previous model of group representation is therefore: (1) the incapacity of constituencies to act as agents; and (2) the incapacity of territory to capture many of people's most significant interests. And yet representative systems based on territory remain everywhere the norm. This means that individuals and groups, especially (but not only) those who are the electoral losers in their own district, are increasingly turning to representatives with whom they identify, but have no electoral relationship, to help advance their interests, whether material or value-based (Mansbridge 2003). We thus see within formally territorial representational systems increasing signs of individuals identifying with representatives who are not accountable to them in any traditional way. This is one of the unavoidable tensions of conventional democratic politics.

The different models of group representation we have discussed in this chapter provide a framework for thinking about how to understand political representation at the constituency level. But none of them can make sense of political representation on their own. Political representation also needs to be understood in its own terms and that means trying to understand what we mean when we talk about representation at the level of the state itself.

Part III
The Politics of Representation

5
Representing the State

So far we have explored the concept of representation in two separate ways: historically, as an idea that evolved to help create the modern state, and subsequently to be shaped by it; and analytically, as an idea that can be understood through a variety of different models, each of which has a range of possible applications. Now is the time to bring these two approaches together and to ask which analytical model best makes sense of the representation of the state as it now exists. In the previous two chapters, we deliberately avoided spelling out some of the full political implications of the different models of representation in order not to prejudge a number of important political questions. The most important of these questions is whether the state is something that can be represented in its own right – and if so, how? – or whether it should simply be regarded as the institutional arrangement that allows for the representation of diverse groups of individuals. The state can be understood both as a group in its own right, in need of representation, and also as the place where the representatives of different groups fight it out amongst themselves (though, if this is to be a successfully functioning state, without violence). The concept of representation can accommodate both these possibilities. What we need to know, and what this chapter will explore, is which of them, or which combination of them, best fits the way we want to do politics.

In what follows we will look at what a range of different theorists have said about representation at the level of the state. Some of these accounts clearly parallel aspects of the historical story we told in the first two chapters; others are new and reflect the analytical possibilities we have explored in the previous two chapters. In drawing together the historical and analytical accounts, a few preliminary remarks may be helpful. The first point to make is that both the history of the concept of representation and an analysis of its uses shows what a varied concept it is, capable of multiple different applications. It is important to distinguish between two kinds of variety here, however. On the one hand, there is the variety that derives from the range of different possible models of representation that can be used – delegation, trusteeship, identity, etc. On the other hand, there is the variety contained *within* each of these different models, since any form of representation will have to allow for both a presence and an absence on the part of the represented and much will depend on which takes priority.

As a result, there can be no definitive answer to the question of what we mean by representation when talking about the state. It will always be possible to conceive of an alternative model to the model we choose. And for any model we choose, there will always be some uncertainty as to what it entails, given the capacity of any model of representation to point in different directions. Representation is a concept that resists being pinned down and that is as true of state representation as of any other kind. But one thing that may be distinctive about states is their capacity to exploit these ambiguities and make full use of them. The historical story certainly seems to suggest this – the state does not fix the idea of representation so much as show what can be done with it, in all its variety. So we need to be careful not to assume that deciding what kind of representation best suits the state means avoiding any ambiguity in our answers; it may be that the ambiguity of representation is one of the things that enables states to function successfully.

The second point is that it is impossible to discuss state representation without introducing the question of legitimacy. In one sense, the question of what makes a particular form of representation legitimate applies to any institution. But in the case of the state, the notion of legitimacy is central for two reasons. First, other bodies can have the legitimacy of their representation determined by the state: if we want to know who is the legitimate representative of a corporation, for example, we can turn to the courts to provide an answer. But the representation of the state itself, though increasingly subject to legal considerations, cannot be reduced to them. It must have some extra-legal dimension, if only because the representatives of the state need a legitimate claim to make the law as well as being subject to it. Second, the legitimacy of state representation is not simply a matter of deciding what entitles particular representatives to speak on behalf of the group. State representatives also need to justify why their form of representation should take priority over other kinds. State representation has claims to legitimacy that transcend those of other groups (and if it doesn't, then it should lead us to question the claims of states to be sovereign, as the political pluralists did). These two points are related and they both go back to Hobbes. States, like other forms of association, depend on representation in order to function at all; but if they are to function specifically as states, with a distinctive claim to represent all their citizens, then they must have a wider claim to legitimacy than other kinds of association.

Where we have moved well beyond Hobbes is in our general expectation that these legitimacy claims will need to be couched in the language of democracy. We increasingly assume that political representation, if it is to be legitimate, must be democratic. The history of representation shows that there is nothing inherently democratic about the idea of representation and that at certain points the two ideas have stood in opposition to each other. At the same time, an analytical account of the different forms of representation shows that it is wrong to impose a false choice between 'direct democracy' on the one hand, and 'representative democracy' on the other. Even direct democracy, in which groups take decisions through the collective decisions of their members, can be understood as a form of representation, given that the majority represents the group as a whole. Equally, even indirect types of representation, such as trusteeship, can involve a form of participation on the part of the members of the group, who may be able to pass judgement on, even if they cannot speak through, the group's representatives.

It is not a question of deciding whether political representation is or is not democratic per se. All democracy relies on some kind of representation and all representation has the potential for some kind of democratic component. The question is how we want to see the fit between democracy and representation. One approach is to decide on certain normative criteria for democracy and then to examine which forms of representation provide the best prospect of meeting these norms. An alternative is to see which model of representation best describes the workings of the state as it has evolved over time and then to ask whether and how this model might be democratized. Either way, applying democratic standards to political representation means that we cannot limit ourselves to simply describing the various possibilities allowed by the concept of representation. We have also to consider what representation ought to be in its most politically valuable or sustainable forms. But we must remember that simply saying representation ought to be democratic does not answer that question.

Representing diversity

All modern states contain two distinct groups of people: the rulers – government, sovereign powers, law-makers, the *representatives*; and the ruled – citizens, people, voters, the *represented*. The relationship of representation is what holds these two groups together in a single entity called the state and it is what enables the ruled to exercise some form of control over their rulers. But the nature of that control can vary with two factors: the kind of representation envisaged and the kind of group both the rulers and the ruled are respectively understood to be. A great deal depends on where one starts. In particular, it matters whether one begins with an assumption about the group character of the rulers or the group character of the ruled.

Let's start with the ruled, whose character in most modern states seems fairly clear: they tend to be large and diverse groups of people with some shared characteristics (including a sometimes weaker, sometimes stronger, shared national identity) but with many features that divide them up into separate groupings, identities, interests, capable of being sep-arately represented. It is therefore fairly common to assume that the system of representation appropriate for a modern state must somehow reflect this diversity and allow different sorts of individuals to be represented according to the differ-ences between them. Yet the question remains how a system of representation can best capture those differences. There are at least three distinct possibilities here.

The first, and in many ways least promising, is the system of functional representation described in the previous chapter. On this account, individuals have representatives who can speak for them in accordance with the different social groups to which they belong – economic, cultural, religious – with no particular priority being given to those who represent them politically, i.e., to the representatives of the state. Instead, political representatives must take their turn with these other representatives, so that sometimes it will be church leaders, or trade unionists, or educationalists, rather than always politicians, whose voice is decisive. The appeal of this account is that it allows for representation to be adapted to the requirements of the moment – if a group of individuals needs someone to speak up for them as the victims of eco-nomic injustice, then functional representation allots that role to someone who represents them as economic agents. But the problem is that functional theories of representation have no convincing account of how we should understand the func-tion of the state. If political representation is just one form among many, in what capacity do political representatives speak, and on whose behalf? Once individuals are repre-sented according to their different social roles, there appears to be no place for the state, which is not a social but a quint-essentially political form of association. Carl Schmitt, who misperceived many things about political representation, nonetheless saw this very clearly:

> A pluralist theory is either the theory of state which arrives at the unity of the state by a federalism of social associations or a theory of the dissolution or rebuttal of the state . . . Above

all, it has to be explained why human beings should have to form a governmental association in addition to the religious, cultural, economic and other associations, and what would be its specific meaning. (Schmitt 1996b: 44)

Another way to put this is that functionalist theories of representation do not specify a particular character for the group of individuals who are to act as political representatives because it is not the job of that group to represent diversity. Diversity is represented by the system as a whole. So in this sense, it does not matter if political representation is in the hands of a narrow band of individuals, or perhaps even a single individual, since no politician will be able to claim to represent the people in their entirety. They will always be up against the rival claims of church, trade unionists, etc. But things look very different if we accept Schmitt's criticism – that the state has to have a distinctively political, or coercive, function if it is to have any function at all – but reject his wider argument: that the state should represent the symbolic unity of the people. If states are much more diverse in their make-up than Schmitt recognized, but if Schmitt is right that they are nonetheless *states*, with the sovereign powers that this entails, then it matters greatly what character is assumed by the particular group of individuals who act as their political representatives. The political representatives themselves must somehow embody the diversity of those whom they represent.

There are a number of ways this might be done. Perhaps the most obvious is to construct the representative relationship in mimetic, or simulative terms, and to look for some microcosm of the wider community in the smaller community of the representative body. One inevitable consequence of this will be that the locus of political representation will be in an assembly, rather than in a single leader or figurehead. Just as medieval popes could represent the unity of the church, but only councils could represent its diversity, so modern parliaments can represent the diversity of modern states much better than modern presidents or prime ministers. Indeed, as we have seen, assemblies can be purposefully constructed to contain a cross-section of the wider population, under systems of proportional representation with quotas specifying that a certain number of representatives must come from particular ethnic minorities, or that a fixed number of representatives must be women. Quotas of this kind are increasingly common in the constitutional arrangements of various new democracies, for example in Rwanda, and also more recently in Iraq. It can also be done informally, as in the United States, where gerrymandering can create constituencies with majority black populations that are therefore more likely to elect black representatives to Congress.

But whether formal or informal, any attempt to produce a representative assembly that better mirrors the wider population runs up against certain practical difficulties. The essential problem is that assemblies are never simply mirrors – they are also decision-making bodies that fulfil an active as well as a simply mimetic role. The mirroring effect of mimetic representation, which may better allow individuals to identify with particular representatives within the assembly, does little to guarantee that the decisions taken by the assembly as a whole will reflect the diversity of the wider community. In some cases, a diverse representative assembly may stand in the way of effective decision-making, particularly if separate groups are able to exercise a form of veto over joint decisions (this has been the result in Iraq). Alternatively, a diverse assembly may simply serve as a cover for more traditional forms of politics, with representatives identifiable according to quotas but still voting along party lines. It may even be counter-productive. There is evidence from the United States that the creation of constituencies designed to guarantee enhanced black representation in Congress, while increasing the number of minority representatives, has actually diminished the responsiveness of Congress as a whole to the interests of minority constituents (Lublin 1997). It appears that giving minorities their 'own' representatives, without additional constitutional guarantees, can simply make it easier for the majority to ignore them.

This potential gap between representation as visible 'presence' and representation as decisive action suggests an alternative model of pluralism: one that reflects diversity not within the assembly itself but in the interaction between the members of the assembly and the claims of competing minority interests that exist outside of it (Dahl 1971, 1991). On this account, various interest groups pressurize representatives to uphold their interests and their success depends on how much pressure they are able to apply and in what form (through lobbying, financial donations, and so on). The representatives themselves do not necessarily, or even usually, share an identity with those on whose behalf they end up acting: they are, for the most part, independent agents, who offer their services to those groups that are able to offer them something in return. A system of this kind revolves around the interplay between two types of representative: the representatives of various interest groups (lobbyists, etc.), who act as agents for their group principals; and elected representatives, who may be constrained by party affiliation and the need to get re-elected but are nonetheless free to take decisions on behalf of whomever it suits them to do so.

Pressure group politics is one way of ensuring that different groups can get heard at different times. But although a broadly pluralist conception of political representation, it nonetheless raises an obvious question: who will speak for the people who find themselves unable to apply the right sort of pressure? Pluralism of this kind is, after all, a form of minority rule, and the fact that different minorities may take it in turns to exercise influence over political representatives does not alter the fact that, at any given moment, the great majority of citizens are excluded. Indeed, any system of representation that prioritizes the influence of small but highly organized interests may in practice prevent cohesive majorities from forming in the first place (Dahl 1971: 18–22). Nor does the inherent pluralism of the system alter the fact that pressure group politics reduces political representation to a form of closed bargaining between an elite group of individuals, many of them acting on their own behalf. For some political theorists, this feature of political life – its dependence on the actions of a self-interested elite – stands in the way of 'genuine' representation because it is so unresponsive to the public at large (Przeworski 1999). But it does not follow that elitist politics is non-representative by definition. As we have seen, representation is an idea that can accommodate self-interest, discretion and the exercise of personal judgement on the part of representatives. What elitism does rule out is the idea that political representation can provide either a mirror of the wider public or a means by which the public as a whole can tell their rulers what to do. In other words, the problem here is not that elitism is inconsistent with the concept of representation. The problem is that it appears to be inconsistent with the idea of democracy.

So we face some fairly stark choices: representative assemblies that reflect the diversity of the public may find themselves relatively powerless to act on that basis; on the other hand, representatives who have the freedom to act also have the freedom to ignore the interests of the public, in all their diversity. Is there any way to close this gap? One possibility, which has garnered a lot of attention in recent years, is to attempt to supplement the workings of representative assemblies with citizen panels or similar deliberative bodies (including citizen juries, 'town hall' meetings, planning cells, consensus conferences and other kinds of deliberative polls) in order to provide some additional representation of the public as it exists outside of the narrow political elite. The attraction of citizen juries lies in their democratic heritage: selecting citizens at random to fulfil significant political roles was a crucial – on some accounts, *the* crucial – feature of Athenian democracy (Manin 1997). One way of thinking about citizen juries in particular is therefore as a democratic alternative to representative politics: these bodies are, for some theorists, the best contemporary exemplars of direct democracy, in that 'the panel members can only represent themselves' (Fixdal 1997: 373). But if citizen juries do not represent anyone except their own members, then it is hard to see how their decisions can hold for anyone except their own members. If they are to fulfil a role that in some sense involves non-members in their decisions, then they must have some kind of representative function. The question is, what kind?

This cannot be representation legitimated by election (since citizen panels are selected rather than elected). Instead, it is more likely to be a form of representation as mimesis, with the panel providing a representative sample of the population as a whole. However, there are at least two different ways of sampling a population: a statistically representative sample replicates the proportionate strength of different groups in the wider population; by contrast, a demographic cross-section might seek to ensure that at least one person from every significant social group is present. How the jury is constructed will depend in large part on what the jury is *for* – whether the central aim is simply to provide an outlet for views that the political process might otherwise have excluded or whether it is to provide a setting in which those with different views can be encouraged to debate the issues and, if necessary, to change their minds. The latter hope is one that is voiced by many deliberative democrats who see citizen juries, 'town hall' meetings and planning cells all as suitable locations for the sort of discussions that might lead to real consensus by means of reasonable argument. But any citizen body in which individual members are given time to inform themselves, to debate among themselves and to change their minds, though it may produce better grounded decisions, raises a problem for that body's representative status. These sorts of structured discussions are by definition atypical of the way most individuals arrive at their political views and therefore the workings of the representative body can no longer be said to 'mirror' society at large. Some other justification for its ability to represent non-members will be needed. The gap between the informed members of a deliberative group and a less well-informed public does not mean that the former cannot represent the latter but it does mean that the language of representation has to shift from a notion of mimesis or 'sampling'.

One way this might be done is through the language of accountability. Though citizen panel members are not accountable to any particular 'constituents', in the sense of being subject to electoral judgement, they will nonetheless have to be accountable for their actions, in the sense of needing to give reasons for the decisions they finally reach (the giving of reasons being the point of deliberative discussions). These reasons can then be presented to the public in order to secure wider approval for a chosen course of action. Indeed, this process of representation through deliberation can be understood as the means by which the possibility of new alliances and constellations of interests among the wider public might emerge (Young 1997). But in the context of conventional electoral politics, once the public is being asked for its approval – for example, through a referendum on the panel's final decision – then a more familiar representative relationship will also come into play. No matter how good the reasons for the panel's decision – no matter how deliberative the discussions that preceded it – the final test of its representativeness will be whether it can command the assent of a population who will not deliberate on the measure in the same way (and, in the case of a referendum, may find that a complex discussion has been turned into a yes-or-no question). The panel is no longer representative of the public simply by being a miniature version of it, taking the sorts of decisions other members of the public might take if they had the time and space to consider them fully and to allow their own views to evolve. It is instead asking the public for its approval. The public may be more likely to approve when it hears the reasoning behind the jury's deliberations. But it may not. Representation that rests on the possibility of objection on the part of the represented is very different from representation understood as a simulation of what the represented might do in similar circumstances. The fundamental difference is that whenever the represented get a chance to voice their objections – in a national vote – the circumstances are no longer similar, since full-blooded electoral competition for votes rarely resembles the careful deliberations of a jury.

There is also the question of the relationship between an assembly of citizens selected to be a sample of the public and the elected representatives chosen by the public to govern them. Governments may pay lip-service to the idea of citizens being allowed to reach their own decisions but, when those decisions conflict with the views of the governing elite, the distinctive 'representativeness' of a citizen jury may not count for much. Citizen juries can be manipulated by those who summon them, their discussions can be skewed towards particular outcomes and the consensus they achieve can be nothing more than the result of group-think. Equally, governments, having summoned them, can choose to ignore them. Some of these problems may be less likely to arise in the case of 'town hall' meetings and other deliberative bodies, which can operate according to their own political dynamic. But the more political these meetings are – in the sense of being more immediately motivated by the pressing political needs of their members – the more likely they are to threaten the government's own claim to be the primary representative of its citizens' political demands. In other words, different modes of representation can, and almost certainly will, clash within the setting of the state.

The example of citizen juries illustrates that any claim by a representative body to speak for the people in all their diversity must always exist in the context of alternative and competing claims, often founded on a very different understanding of what representation entails. As well as being represented by a cross-section of its members, the public can also be represented by a majority of its members (as in a referendum), and by those a wide range of its members have elected to represent them (as in a parliament). In the case of a citizen jury, the representation of diversity will be a significant part of its claims to legitimacy. However, in the case of majority decision it is not the assumption of diversity but of unity among the represented that grounds the representative process: the public is represented as though capable of speaking with a single voice. In the case of elected assemblies, both diversity and unity can be represented. Parliaments and other legislative bodies are capable of reflecting the different voices, identities and interests that make up the wider community; but they are also capable of giving that community a single voice, and acting on its behalf as though it were a single agent. Even when parliament is understood as a primarily deliberative body – as it was by John Stuart Mill and has been more recently by theorists such as Iris Marion Young and Nadia Urbinati – it can still seek to transform diversity into unity by providing a new perspective on familiar differences that enables such differences to be overcome. There is therefore another potential clash we need to consider: between the representation of diversity and the representation of the state as a unified whole.

Representing unity

The most straightforward contrast to seeing the state as an amalgam of diverse groups of individuals is to see it as a unified entity in its own right, capable of acting as a principal, and therefore capable of appointing political representatives to act as its agents. This is a view with a long heritage, as we have seen, stretching back to Rousseau and beyond. But as we have also seen, it is at odds with the prevailing tradition of state representation. The idea that a political community possesses its own 'will', in a way that allows it to dictate the actions of its representatives, depends on a particular conception of what a political community is, and how it operates: it must be relatively small, relatively homogenous, with active citizens ready both to participate in collective decision-making and to maintain a vigilant eye on their representatives to keep them in line. This might describe an idealized version of the medieval city-state, and it certainly describes Rousseau's ideal version of a modern republic (in which a government is meant to act literally as the 'agent' of a sovereign people), but it does not describe the real world of modern politics. Modern states are too large, modern citizens too diverse (not simply in their various interests but in the varying level of their interest in politics) and modern politicians too much of a professional elite for governments plausibly to act as the people's 'agents' (let alone, in Tony Blair's memorable phrase, as the 'servants of the people'). There is simply no satisfactory way for modern citizenries to keep their governments under control, even though new information technology means governments are increasingly sensitized to shifts in the public mood. The best the public can still hope to achieve is to keep the behaviour of their representatives under review, to keep them worrying about re-election and if necessary to get rid of them when the opportunity arises. Schumpeter may have been wrong both about Rousseau and the theory of representation but he was surely right about this.

However, it does not follow that the public of a modern state can never be represented as having a coherent will of its own. What it means is that this will has to be discovered in the act of representation itself – or in Schumpeter's more reductive terms, it has to be 'manufactured'. There are a number of ways this might be done. One is to construct a system of representation that is deliberately designed to enhance or identify those moments of concord of which even the most dispersed publics are sometimes capable. Andrew Rehfeld, for instance, has proposed abandoning territorial representation altogether in order to achieve a more dynamic form of majoritarian politics (see Rehfeld 2005). In his view, we should move beyond pseudo-conceptions of localized interest, identity and agency to embrace more explicit randomness by assigning voters randomly into constituencies which will be theirs for life. Like a random statistical sample, such constituencies would be microcosms of the whole nation. The consequence is that each representative will represent a cross-section of the nation and what is good for his or her constituency should correspond to what is good for the nation as a whole. The point of a system like this would be to cut across those ties of minority interest that may become entrenched under conventional schemes of constituency representation. Random constituencies would be more responsive to shifts in popular opinion, without being subject to the breaks of sectional or minority representation. When a government becomes unpopular, it would become unpopular in every single constituency.

The attraction of this conception of representation lies in its ability to track and then reflect the views of the national majority. But it remains a somewhat crude device and a highly artificial form of unity. It is still a constituency-based scheme of representation, and therefore presupposes a certain amount of independence on the part of the representatives (if not, then it would make more sense to put decisions out directly to majority vote by means of regular referenda). Representatives who are answerable to randomly generated constituencies will in some respects need to be more independent than the representatives of geographical constituencies. This is because anyone who represents a microcosm of the nation, but chooses to go against the majority view, will by definition be prioritizing his or her own judgement. By contrast, the representatives of localities can always justify a decision to side with the minority on the grounds that they are standing up for the interests of their constituents (as will be the case whenever a local majority forms part of a national minority). So randomly generated constituencies may actually open up a new gap between representatives and represented: if the public is to be represented in its diversity as well as its moments of unity, it will be by representatives who no longer speak for those who elected them.

Another way to capture the unity of the public within a scheme of representation is to look beyond the representation of interests and towards other kinds of shared perspectives. For example, Brennan and Hamlin have suggested that the concept of representation should not simply be viewed through the prism of the voters' interests, nor judged according to its responsiveness to those interests. Whenever it is seen in these reductive terms, representation will always emerge as a second-best option to direct democracy because the interests of the representatives will inevitably get in the way of majority preferences (Brennan and Hamlin 1999). But representative politics can be responsive to more than simply the interests of individual voters. It can also be, in Brennan and Hamlin's terms, 'expressive', meaning that it can be a device for individuals to express their views of the political process as a whole and of the merits of the various actors within it.

Brennan and Hamlin offer the following analogy:

> The voters are like fans at a football game: they can choose to cheer for one team or the other, but they cannot choose the result of the game, and no one individual's act of cheering has any significant effect on the result. If we wish to explain who or what citizens choose to vote for, we need to look at the considerations that will induce expressions of support, rather than individual voter's particularized interests. (Ibid.: 118)

Among the things that the voters may express in the act of voting is their view of the capacity of their representatives to judge what is in the public interest – in other words, of their merit or virtues as decision-makers. If the public interest is reduced to the sum total of the interests of its individual members, then anything that their representatives do is bound to be disappointing. But if the members of the public are asked to express a view about how their representatives are performing or likely to perform as interpreters of their shared interests, then they may be able to reach a collective judgement independently of all the differences of individual interest that might otherwise divide them. Representation can be a means of overcoming the differences between individuals and their interests, once it is seen as something more than just a reflection of them.

On this account, the public interest becomes a product of the system of representative politics, rather than a precondition of it. It does not emerge from voter preferences; instead, voters tend to prefer those representatives who do the best job of bringing the public interest into view. In this respect, there are parallels with the views of those deliberative democrats who see the process of deliberation as itself creating a consensus that can then be represented back to the wider public. Brennan and Hamlin's version of this argument belongs to the idiom of rational choice theory and is designed to show that it is rational to vote even though voting offers the individual voter no direct input into the political process (like many rational choice theorists, they want an answer to the question of why anyone should bother to vote at all). Expressive voting provides the electorate with a good reason to vote because it permits a form of involvement in politics that offers rewards beyond having direct input in a given outcome. To slightly alter the terms of Brennan and Hamlin's analogy, it turns the voters into an audience who can help to determine the success of a performance by supplying their applause (or alternatively, can doom a performance by withholding it) but who cannot direct the action as it takes place on the stage. Yet once the analogy is put in these terms, it suggests a very different idiom through which to understand the business of political representation, one in which conceptions of agency drawn from aesthetics and drama rather than economics are the key.

'Aesthetic' theories of political representation, though very different in style and inspiration from the rational choice approach, nevertheless share some presuppositions with the 'expressive' theory described above. There is an agreement between these two accounts that a naive principal–agent conception of political representation is inadequate to describe the role of the electorate in appointing representatives because the interests of the voters do not cohere in such a way as to make them a plausible principal. There is also a shared sense that any community of interests among the voters is more plausibly a product of the system of representation than a precondition for it. Where aesthetic conceptions of political representation go further is in borrowing from the world of art the idea that any form of representation is never simply the copy of some pre-existing external reality. In aesthetic terms, representation always creates something new.

So, for example, a painting of a landscape never simply replicates that landscape; it creates a new version of it in the act of representing it. Likewise, stage actors do not represent characters as they might exist off the stage; stage actors bring their characters to life in the act of representing them. There is thus always a 'gap' between an object and the representation of that object and this holds in politics as well. Political representatives can never merely speak for the views or interests of the people as they existed before being represented; instead, by definition, the act of representing them creates a new version of the people and their interests, and it is this creativity that marks out political representation as a dynamic form of politics. As Frank Ankersmit, one of the most prominent exponents of an 'aesthetic' theory of political representation, has argued, any attempt to close the gap between the people and their representatives is futile (Ankersmit 1997). Indeed, he has suggested that the attempt to establish mimetic forms of identity between rulers and ruled is 'not the realization of democracy but an invitation to tyranny' because it thwarts any opportunity for the people to reflect on and judge the actions of their representatives. Political representation is not designed to provide a reflection of the people and their interests; rather it is designed to give the people an image of themselves to reflect on.

Unlike rational choice theorists, Ankersmit is not interested in trying to uncover the underlying rationality behind this arrangement. Nor is he primarily interested in the question of why individuals vote at all. The focus of his account is historical; it explores the ways in which political institutions have developed within the gap that representation opens up between government and people and the ways in which history itself constitutes a series of representations of political reality (Ankersmit 2002). A similar interest lies at the heart of the work of the French political theorist Claude Lefort, who like a number of his compatriots (notably Pierre Rosanvallon) has used the history of the French republic to illustrate the open-endedness of the concept of representation and the permanent state of tension that exists between the represented and their representatives.

In contrast to Ankersmit, Lefort focuses less on analogies between political and aesthetic representation and concentrates instead on the particular tension that emerges within the concept of representation whenever it is 'democratized' (something that has been taking place, in Lefort's terms, ever since the French Revolution). For Lefort, there is a paradox at the heart of the idea of 'representative democracy'. The democratization of the political process – which includes the expansion of the franchise, the entrenchment of individual rights and the rise of public opinion – has given the public a greater and more active part to play in the institutions of representative government. But as the public's role expands, so the public's identity becomes more fractured because the more actively the public is involved in its own representation, the more clearly the divisions and dislocations among its individual members are revealed. Democracy, in this sense, has made it harder to represent the people as a whole. Lefort writes:

> Nothing makes the paradox of democracy more palpable than the institution of universal suffrage. It is at the very moment when popular sovereignty is assumed to manifest itself, when the people is assumed to actualize itself by expressing its will, that social interdependence breaks down and that the citizen is abstracted away from all the networks in which his social life develops and becomes a mere statistic. Number replaces substance. (Lefort 1988: 18–19)

For Lefort, this analysis points to an 'emptiness' at the core of representative democracy where the people ought to be: the same processes that bring the people into focus as a single political agent are also the processes that lead to the dissolution of the people. But there is another way to put this. In any system of representative democracy, there will always be more than one version of the people at work. There is 'the people' conjured up by representatives in the act of speaking for them; and there are the 'people' who pass judgement on these conjuring acts, often in ways that give the lie to them, but who nevertheless see themselves as members of the body politic as a whole (see figure 5.1). It does not necessarily follow that these two different kinds

Figure 5.1 Representing the people

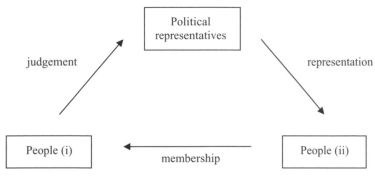

of people will always be in conflict with each other. Sometimes political representatives will seek to embody a sense of national unity that finds a direct echo in the electorate. But it does mean that the potential for conflict is always there.

Indeed, the functioning of representative democracy depends upon politicians being able to offer competing visions *of* the people *to* the people, in order for the voters to be able to choose the one they prefer. No single one of these visions will ever succeed in closing the gap between the represented and their representatives entirely. Moreover, the more successful a particular vision is in closing that gap, the more scope there will be for dissenting politicians to point up the ways in which a close identification between rulers and ruled effectively excludes the people from politics in their active, or judgemental, role. One just has to think of what can happen to representative democracies during wartime – a strong sense of national unity may result in widespread acquiescence in the actions of the people's representatives and therefore the suspension of democratic competition. But when the war is over, the people may react sharply against the assumption that they are happy to identify with their leaders and can be taken for granted. This is effectively what happened in Britain in 1945 when the people voted Churchill out of office and elected a Labour government by a landslide.

Lefort's account of political representation, like Ankersmit's, does not sit easily with some of the assumptions that we like to make about representative democracy. In particular, it makes it difficult to assume that a system of representation is more democratic the more the people play an active role within it. In any system of representation, the active and passive roles of the people are always present and always in some degree of tension with one another. This means that the representation of the people is, in a sense, permanently up for grabs. The fluidity and indeterminacy of this conception of political representation also makes it hard to square with some other forms of academic enquiry, above all with the kind of political theory or political science that seeks to pin representation down and define it in unambiguous terms. Theories of representation that highlight its 'gaps' or its 'emptiness' can be dismissed as woolly or even empty themselves by hard-nosed theorists who want something more concrete. Certainly it is true that 'continental' and 'analytical' theories of political representation rarely engage with one another. But that does not mean that they do not overlap.

As we have seen, the problem of establishing a clear identity for the people as principal is one that is felt by rational choice theorists and deliberative democrats as well as continental philosophers and historians. Equally, the notion that the voters have more than one part to play within a system of representative government – as both the objects of representation and the arbiters of that representation – is hard to dispute in any idiom. Hanna Pitkin, who remains the most widely cited theorist of representation in the political science literature, accepts that representation is an inherently 'paradoxical' idea (Pitkin 1967). Bernard Manin, who is French but also himself a political scientist, acknowledges that representation is necessarily 'Janus-faced' (Manin 1997). It does not follow from this that the representation of the people is therefore an illusion, nothing more than a trick of the light that we ought to be able to see through. Lefort is not suggesting this any more than Pitkin or Manin is. But it does mean that any unity that is achieved through a system of representative democracy will be subject to dispute within the very terms of that system.

Unity vs. diversity

The account of popular representation given in the previous section cannot be reduced to any one of the analytical models of group representation discussed in chapter 4. Clearly it does not fit a straightforward principal–agent model because the 'people' that emerges from the act of representation is not the same as the 'people' who appoint and dismiss representatives – the principal, if there is one here, is not what is being represented by the agent. Nor can this picture easily be reconciled with the idea of representation as a form of identity politics because what people identify with is something that emerges from the representative process itself rather than something that can be fed into it. If anything, this account is closest to representation as trusteeship, particularly as that model connects to the idea of the representation of corporate 'fictions'. The representation of the people is the representation of a fiction, in so far as what is being represented does not exist except through being represented. Nevertheless, the legalistic origins of the trustee model do not suit either the dynamism or the uncertainty of democratic politics. Legally authorized trustees are free to exercise their own judgement within the terms of the trust given them. But elected representatives in modern states have constantly to renegotiate the terms of that trust with the people who have the power to hire and fire them. The people may be a fiction in one sense; but in another sense, certainly so far as the politicians are concerned, the power of the people is all too real.

So perhaps we should say that in a treatment like Lefort's, representative democracy can be viewed as a form of politics that accommodates aspects of each of these different models. The people have an active role, as the arbiters of representation, much like principals. The people also have a passive role, as the objects of representation, much like legal fictions. And in judging in their active role what they think of the image offered of them by their representatives, individual voters will often side with those representatives with whom they identify best. Any system of representation will contain elements of these different models and how they interact with each other will go a long way to determining how the state evolves over time. For Lefort, it is this scope for tension and conflict between different conceptions of representation that helps to make sense of the historical development of the state, through periodic crises and more gradual shifts in the interactions between rulers and ruled. The turbulent history of the French state, in particular, can be explained by the fact that it is a 'representative' state, and representation, far from closing down questions about the appropriate role of the people in their government, always leaves such questions open.

However, if we look at other, relatively more stable systems of representative government, a slightly different picture emerges. The United States and Great Britain have evolved systems of representative government that include both active and passive forms of popular representation and allow for the representation of the people both as a unified whole and as a set of diverse individuals. However, the two systems have struck a somewhat different balance between these different forms of representation. As Philip Pettit has recently argued (Pettit 2006), the Washington model places greater emphasis on what he calls the 'enactive' representation of constituencies and interest groups by individual representatives ('enactive' here meaning the representation of principals by agents). In Congress, individual representatives are primarily answerable to separate constituencies and as a result there is also a 'simulative' (or what we might otherwise call 'mimetic') component to the legislature, in that the diversity of the population is reflected in the differences between the members of the House (though this is not 'mimesis' in the fullest sense of meaning a replication of the wider population – there are not nearly enough women, or blacks, or Hispanics in the upper reaches of American politics for that). Meanwhile, the representation of the people as a whole tends to devolve on to the office of the President who must then act in conjunction with Congress in order to get various measures into law. So corporate representation is often a fractured business (except in times of war or national emergency), depending on transient coalitions of interests. National political parties, though they are crucial in getting individuals elected, are often not strong enough to hold those individual representatives to a single vision of the popular interest.

In the Westminster model, by contrast, political parties stand for election on manifesto commitments that are more or less expected to be binding on all constituency representatives. As Pettit puts it: 'In this system, the individual-level representation of constituency gets put in a decidedly second place, since individual members will vote as their party votes and will be expected even by those who elect them to vote that way.' But, he goes on: 'If that is the weakness of the system, the strength is that the parliament as a whole will operate very efficiently to generate a body of legislation that can be expected to be internally coherent, and to cohere with established law and principle' (Pettit 2006: 26). In other words, parliament tries (or at least affects) to legislate for the people as a corporate body and it acts itself as a corporate body to that end.

To put it crudely, the Westminster model prioritizes the representation of unity over diversity and the Washington model, the representation of diversity over unity. But this is, inevitably, much too crude because both systems allow for both kinds of representation, depending on circumstances. The President can speak for the American people in ways that trump local loyalties and a British MP can speak for her constituents in ways that trump loyalty to the national party. Under either system there will always be conflicts between the representation of unity and the representation of diversity and both systems are designed to permit such conflicts while attempting to render them manageable. So perhaps it would be better to say that the frustrations of each system reflect where the balance between them lies. Members of the British electorate are more likely to think that their representatives don't represent them personally but serve the party machine. Members of the American electorate are more likely to think that their representatives are prisoners of special interests and don't see the wider picture.

These frustrations spill out into another feature of any system of representative government where the public are free to express their dissatisfaction with their elected representatives: the existence of 'representatives' of the public who operate outside the electoral system (and outside of deliberately constructed schemes intended to give the public a voice, such as citizen panels). Among those who may claim to represent the public, or sections of the public, are journalists, campaigners, charity workers, celebrities, or simply members of the public who have been thrust into the limelight. These are not principal–agent relationships, though they are sometimes dressed up in similar terms. Newspapers sometimes claim that they are empowered to speak on behalf of their readers – the British tabloid *The Sun* likes to dress up its political campaigns as being on behalf of '*Sun* readers' – but the act of buying a newspaper is hardly sufficient to ground a principal–agent relationship. The representatives of NGOs do act as agents for their particular organization (particularly when they are its employees) but that does not mean they are the agents of those they are trying to help who often, being poor or vulnerable or excluded, lack the kind of agency needed to get a foothold in the political system.

This means that such claims to represent the excluded are invariably grounded in a mixture of simulation and trusteeship – these sorts of informal representatives are either assumed to be speaking for those who cannot speak for themselves or speaking for those who would say the same were they in a position to speak out. Either way, what grounds claims to representation from outside the electoral system is a sense that conventional politics, on whatever model it is organized, leaves some people lacking in representation and that these people need to be spoken for. As the rock singer Bono once put it, to justify his having taken on the cause of the African poor: 'I represent a lot of people [in Africa] who have no voice at all . . . They haven't asked me to represent them. It's cheeky but I hope they're glad I do' (O'Neill 2005).

The example of Bono and Africa illustrates a number of important features of this sort of representation. It shows that the lack of specific authorization – the fact that 'they haven't asked [him]' – is a potentially serious handicap because no claims to represent exist in isolation. They must always compete with rival claims and even those who lack a voice do not lack rivals purporting to speak for them. In particular, there are always states which, for all their obvious inability to speak for all the people all the time, nonetheless have evolved in a way that gives them a particular claim to represent their peoples. The power of states rests on their ability to accommodate the many different varieties of representation we have discussed so far in this book, including not just trusteeship and identity politics but also the authority that comes through popular election. As we saw in the previous chapter, it is hard for other kinds of representatives to compete with this. Both experts and activists, the two groups outside government that tend to speak out for others, rely on knowledge and passion to generate perspectives that are not, for the most part, those shared by the majority of us. Campaigners lack the specific authority claims of political representatives and have to rely on claims of identity or shared interest that may be unstable or transient. Newspapers will often discomfort governments by speaking up for their readers but they will still have to wait either for the governments to act or for their readers (in conjunction with others) to get rid of the government. The durability of the system of state representation, in all its various guises, is a testimony to the breadth of the vision of representative government for which it allows.

But Bono's claim to speak for the poor of Africa takes us beyond the nation-state. It rests on two other, relatively novel, features of political representation. First, in some parts of the world the state has failed, or is failing, to represent its citizens. However well the state may be able to represent individuals in theory, in practice some states lack even the basic rudiments of power needed to make their representation claims plausible. The 'gap' between the represented and their political representatives is just too wide. In these circumstances, the representation provided by alternative bodies, including NGOs and other kinds of international organizations, may become, and may need to become, more significant. Second, even the successful and stable states of the affluent West are increasingly finding themselves constrained by transnational schemes or networks in which their representative status is being reconfigured. States are subject to new sorts of limitations on their ability to speak for their citizens. Some of these limitations derive from the expansion of the role of international law. Others derive from the wide range of international bodies in which states must themselves be represented and through which they can find themselves spoken for. These new constraints – or opportunities – for political representation in the international sphere, between and beyond states, are the subject of the next chapter.

6
Representation Beyond the Nation-State

For most of the history of modern politics, arguments about political representation have revolved around the state. But from the second half of the twentieth century on, state representation has increasingly had to co-exist with the various other forms of political representation that have been proliferating outside it. These involve both interstate and non-state agencies, and raise questions parallel to those we saw arising within states, concerning rival claims to representation but at a higher level of complexity. This additional complexity arises for two main reasons. First, international groups are by definition more complex than national groups, if only because they contain different nationalities among their members. Second, representative politics at the international level introduces a new dimension to the competition to represent the citizens of nation-states. This is the competition that may arise between states and rival claimants to their role as the ultimate arbiter of their citizens' interests.

However, it is important not to be premature in announcing the death of the state at the hands of a wider vision of globally representative politics. International competition between rival agencies does not necessarily spell the end of the state's pre-eminence as a representative institution. Indeed, this may be a competition that states, with all their experience of how representation works, are well equipped to win. Despite the challenge globalization poses to the state's claim to be the sole legitimate representative of the public interest within its given territory, states are still the primary locus of decision-making authority, which they can choose to delegate internationally.

Moreover, besides threatening the scope nation-states have for independent action, the process of globalization has also brought states closer together in the attempt to grasp the benefits of collaboration as members of international organizations and governmental networks. The different institutional entities that perform the basic functions of states – legislation, adjudication, implementation, etc. – are increasingly reaching out to their foreign and supranational counterparts to solve collective problems that spill beyond their borders. This means that states can disaggregate into their component institutions, for certain purposes, but still act as unitary actors when necessary. Moreover, their component parts, when interacting with counterparts across borders, still represent national interests in various ways (Slaughter 2004). Twenty-first century politics is therefore unlikely to signal the end of the state's representative role. But it may well see a shift in emphasis in the sort of representation states provide, and the sort of representation they expect, as they themselves become the principals of multiple international agents.

Besides changes in their external relations, states are also being transformed internally in ways that are relevant for trans-border representation. Immigration has changed radically many states' social, ethnic and cultural make-up. Non-white people whose first language is not English now make up a greater percentage of the US population than at any other time in its history. Today, Muslims constitute the majority of immigrants in most Western European countries, including Belgium, France, Germany and the Netherlands, and the largest single component of the immigrant population in the United Kingdom itself. As a result, immigrant communities will sometimes indirectly represent the interests of foreign nationals, in particular if these are likely to be affected by the policies of their host countries (for example, recent French policy towards Iraq showed a particular sensibility to Muslim opinion). Any claim to represent the interests of people in their countries of origin, or in larger cultural communities, such as the worldwide Muslim brotherhood, is usually based on a shared identity. This is especially so with regard to first-generation immigrants whose ties to the communities of origin are stronger. But the claim is also advanced by their disaffected offspring who, despite being born and socialized in a new country, feel that they are citizens in name only. Still, the latter's claim to represent on the basis of identity is deeply problematic. Their actions are a manifestation of modern identity politics, fuelled by their sense of being stuck between two cultures, neither of which they can fully identify with. So they may quite simply be representing no one but themselves against the state and protesting against its incapacity to offer post-ethnic forms of national citizenship and belonging.

But whatever their provenance, and whether or not they are evidence of disaffection or of a more profound shift in political values, it is clear that states face new challenges. Cross-border policy issues – from the environment to terrorism, from financial risk to immigration – can no longer be tackled through unilateral state action. They demand structures of international governance promoting closer cooperation between the representatives of different states. Moreover, states have not only delegated power upwards to international organizations, they have also started to devolve power downwards to regions. In the process, both sub- and supranational territorial units, especially regions and regional blocs, have asserted themselves as an important subset of the numerous new actors involved in representation beyond borders. At the same time, the speeding up of global communications, combined with the fact that many decisions that affect our lives are now taken across borders, have opened up a new space for trans-national political action by non-state actors. Global social movements, trans-national advocacy networks, global public policy networks and international non-governmental organizations (NGOs) are amongst the many new 'civil society' representatives of an increasingly mobilized world public.

As the number, and the diversity, of trans-national actors has increased, so have the forms of international representation. Several international organizations (IOs) now combine the representation of state actors with non-state actors, such as NGOs. Many different types of groups, from interest groups to more fluid collections of people who band together to pursue some far-reaching social goal (i.e., social 'networks' or 'movements'), have found alternative sites of representation, in multiple institutional and non-institutional venues, such as festivals, sit-ins, protest marches, or cyber-forums. These different categories of representation, ranging from the traditional delegation of state power to the representation of new kinds of global communities, can blend into one another. State alliances, for instance, can create the possibility of collective representation of communities of interest that spread across borders. This is potentially the case with the International Criminal Court: although it was created on the basis of a treaty joined by 105 states, it acts not as a bound agent of those states but rather as an independent trustee of the victims of genocide and war crimes around the world.

Underlying all these developments is the fact that we live in an increasingly connected world. But there is an important caveat here when the discussion centres, as ours does, on representation. A 'connected' world does not automatically entail a new world of representation. Ironically, perhaps, one of those who might view this differently is Sieyès, the architect of nationalism as the basis of representative government. Sieyès conceptualized the division of labour as an advantageous system of mutual representation, where each person should have as much work as possible done on his behalf by specialized 'others'. In Sieyès's scheme of 'representative labour', the workers who produce my tennis shoes in a sweatshop in Indonesia, for instance, have been working, unknowingly, as my representatives.

But Sieyès notwithstanding, it is a mistake to use the term 'representation' simply as a synonym for mutual connectivity. Representation, as we have seen in chapter 3, requires something more than working for another's benefit. To qualify as my 'representative', someone must be acting for me in relation to others, in ways that implicate me in what he or she does and make me in some sense responsible for his or her actions. This is clearly not the case with the Indonesian sweatshop workers. I have no presence in their actions and certainly no presence I can assert, especially in cases of misrepresentation. For there is no place for misrepresentation here: the Indonesian workers may be subject to the will of others – they may be controlled in conditions of near servitude – but that does not make them anyone else's representative (except, perhaps, as symbols of injustice). If anything, representation is something they are likely to experience in their lives as a lack. The world in which we live may well be increasingly interconnected. But an increase in connectivity does not necessarily mean an increase in representation.

If globalization does not itself produce more representation, what it has increased is the demand for representation, particularly within the institutions of global governance, where that demand has never been greater. It has also enhanced the quest for more informal ways of representing 'communities' of identity, interest, value or opinion across national boundaries. If anything, globalization has made representation more central to world politics, while making it less clear how it is to be achieved. The interconnectedness of modern social life inevitably ties the actions of people and institutions in one country to consequences that stem from other countries' people and institutions. And yet no person can be present at all the decisions, or in all those international decision-making bodies, whose actions affect their lives (see Young 2000). Their presence in those decisions depends acutely on the interaction between a variety of institutional and non-institutional sites of representation which bring people together, across borders, in various different ways.

Non-governmental representation

From the 1970s on we have witnessed a global efflorescence of non-governmental politics, questioning the state's exclusive ability to represent society in international relations. Operating as counterweights to states, non-governmental agencies and activists of very different geographical and ideological outlooks have sought to establish themselves in the role of accountability and advocacy agencies. Whether speaking on behalf of the environment, the economically enslaved, the interests of multinational corporations' stakeholders (workers, suppliers, consumers, etc.), those dependent on humanitarian aid, or the victims of violations of human rights, they have become a major force in world politics.

For some commentators, this rise of non-governmental politics is proof that 'politics extends beyond the realm of representation' (Feher 2007: 26). On this account, representation is identified as the distinctive business of states, tied to traditional state-based activities, such as the competition between rival political elites, and limited by their ultimate accountability to national electorates. The point of non-governmental politics is to get beyond this and to find new ways of doing politics that do not depend on narrow forms of electoral accountability. But this is itself too narrow a conception of representation. The notion that non-governmental politics, which aims at transcending the state, must also repudiate representation, the main instrument of state politics, rests on too restricted an understanding of what representation requires.

According to the advocates of a post-representative non-governmental politics, if non-governmental agencies or activists make a claim to represent international groups, involving multiple nationalities, they will simply produce a shallow or empty version of the politics they are trying to get away from. This is because non-governmental agencies are 'deprived of the authority bestowed on elected officials, which makes them vulnerable to the accusation of being neither representative nor accountable' (Feher 2007: 15). In these terms, NGOs need to leave representation behind and find alternative sources of legitimacy and/or accountability.

But there are two problems here. First, representation goes well beyond narrow conceptions of legitimacy, and certainly beyond those centring exclusively on elections, which function both to authorize representatives and to hold them to account. The internal diversity of the concept of representation, as explored in previous chapters, allows for various other ways in which non-governmental agencies can justify their claim to represent trans-national 'constituencies' (these include representation through trusteeship, identity politics, and so on). Indeed, a rival claim to representation is implicit in non-governmental activists' understanding of their activity as a quest to challenge the inadequate presence of the dispossessed in the decision-making procedures of inter-state organizations (like the IMF, the World Bank, the UN). If non-governmental activists were simply speaking interna-tionally on their own behalf, there would be no reason to expect their objections, or indeed their decisions, to hold for anyone other than themselves. If non-members are to be in any way involved in their actions, then NGOs must be exer-cising some broader representative function.

Second, because of the uncertainty and ambiguity at the heart of the concept of representation, it is tempting to believe that non-governmental agencies should turn instead to the notion of accountability. But without representation, account-ability is a fairly narrow idea, certainly narrower than rep-resentation itself. There is no intrinsic value in accountability or, as it is often called, 'transparency'. We may encourage opportunities for deception, and undermine professional per-formance, in our zeal for transparency and heavy-handed forms of accountability (O'Neill 2002). The requirement for more transparency can easily redound, not in openness, but in tighter and more centralized control of information (Hood and Heald 2006). Transparency is thus to be valued instru-mentally as a means to other valued objects sought by public policy. Amongst these is likely to be the representation of the substantive interests of all those likely to be affected by a given policy.

As we have seen in chapter 4, representation need not presuppose the appointment of a representative who has agreed to act on a particular constituency's behalf. It can equally be founded on individuals identifying more widely, possibly across national boundaries, with things they under-stand themselves as having in common: an interest, an ideology, a set of values, a sense of marginalization. So instead of dropping the idea of representation altogether, non-governmental politics needs to re-appropriate it in all its variety. Yet there is a real danger here that too promiscuous use of the idea of representation outside of its traditional context can make it a facile or empty idea. It is not enough for those engaged in trans-national politics to assume that, when they have found a shared interest outside the state, they will by definition have found something they can represent. Representation always depends on something more than mere shared interests – it requires the presence of the represented in the actions of their representatives. Such presence is not automatic in cases of shared interests: it needs to be constructed or worked for. There are, however, a variety of different ways this might be achieved. Some idea of how is given in the examples we discuss next.

Class actions

Because many of the interests people have are diffuse, they are often left unrepresented. Diffuse interests, such as consumer or environmental ones, are interests related to an unspecified community of people who are held together by de facto circumstances. These interests are often unrepresented in the normal political process because the costs to individuals of organizing themselves in large groups, to press for their representation, are not matched by the small gains accruing to each individual from this process. Therefore, the representation of diffuse interests is usually dependent on representative entrepreneurship: someone, or some body, takes the initiative of articulating the interest, thereby mobilizing the relevant group and prompting wider group member identification.

To illustrate: consumer protection legislation recognizes consumer rights but in many cases consumers do not institute judicial proceedings in order to assert their rights, due to the costs of litigation. There is a solution to this and similar problems of collective action, however. A large number of individualized claims can be aggregated into one single representative lawsuit, known as a 'class action'. Some legal representations across borders, especially in the domain of environmental and consumer rights, may suit well the model of 'class action'.

In 2007, a British law firm, representing up to 5,000 local victims, launched a class action over allegedly highly toxic waste dumped in the Ivory Coast from a cargo ship chartered by a London-based company. Its initiative allowed for the representation of foreign nationals by dint of the interests they shared but which they were unable to articulate for themselves. In Europe, the resort to class actions is still limited, especially when compared with the thriving litigation industry established around them in the US. But the situation may be changing rapidly. The European Commission is considering the introduction into the European Union of cross-border 'class actions' suits by consumer organizations. These would enable claims against faulty manufacturers and suppliers in multiple jurisdictions to be aggregated and brought together at a European level. But just as the idea of European class actions is unsurprisingly facing the resistance of corporations, so too is it bound to encounter some resistance from states, particularly when it is directed against their own negligence or that of their officials. States, through their courts, remain responsible for certification of the 'class' in most forms of class action and, in many cases, for certification of who can file the claim on its behalf. Like any form of legal representation, therefore, though it may provide an outlet for those who find themselves unrepresented at the state level, it is unlikely in itself to offer much competition to states. States still control the process.

NGOs, international pressure groups and advocacy networks

As forms of international interest group representation, class actions are often distinguished by being short-lived and self-cancelling, in that the 'class' or 'interest group' ceases to exist as its claim is attended. The same can arguably be said of some other forms of trans-national group representation, such as anti-war coalitions. The end of the war leaves them without their grounds for existence. But in general groups like international pressure groups, advocacy networks or NGOs pull together a more durable set of interests and seek to act on their behalf in an overtly political way – that is, it is part of their *raison d'être* to challenge the representative claims of other organizations. This is because the very object of their actions is often 'bad' or 'unrepresentative' governance, regardless of whether the criticized agency is a state, an IO or a multinational corporation.

The oppositional character of non-governmental politics has two main consequences. First, as unelected groups or individuals, they have to find alternative ways of asserting their own democratic credentials. Second, their representative claims have to compete with those claims put forward by individual states or states coming together in international organizations.

Competing with governmental forms of representation can be daunting. To take the case of NGOs first, their critics frequently accuse them of being autocratic and self-serving organizations, beholden neither to voters, nor to those communities whose interests they seek to promote but, in the best-case scenario, simply to their own financial backers (and, in the worst-case scenario, to no one at all). Lacking in internal democratic procedures, NGOs appear to be less democratic, and less accountable, than the states and IOs they criticize – or so their critics claim.

Underlying this line of criticism is the question of whom NGOs represent, if anyone, and how. Do they represent their members, their donors, the people or things whose cause they champion, or the interests of the international community at large? The answer is not always simple and usually involves a combination of these different kinds of representation.

In many respects, membership-based NGOs are the most straightforward case: the NGO represents, primarily, the views and interests of its members. But the members of such organizations will often see its role not in terms of their own representation, but the representation of some group or cause that they wish to support. Equally, the organization will not simply be accountable to its members – it will also have to answer to those who support it in other ways, including occasional donors, and governments.

NGOs without a direct membership base, such as Oxfam and Christian Aid, both of which are charities, bear a strong resemblance to the corporate model of representation we have analysed in chapter 4. But if anything their case is even more complex. They finance their activity through a variety of sources, including private benefactors, foundations, governmental, EU and UN grants, to each of which they must account for the allocations of their funds. Moreover, these NGOs are run by groups of trustees, who are bound by the expectations of their donors, but they are not supposed to represent such people, or their interests, as their mandate is to act independently of anyone who may be financing them. Directors, as well as lesser officers, ought to serve the interests of the NGO itself, which has a separate legal personality and is an actor in its own right – they are in this sense *its* representatives. They must make the NGO present in their dealings with third parties – government officials, UN agencies, other NGOs, donors and the beneficiaries of their programmes (see figure 6.1).

All of these are potentially relationships of representation, with their own forms of accountability: governments might be represented by NGOs, who will be answerable to them, but governments will also represent individual members (as voters) to whom they will in turn be answerable; employees will act for the organization in some capacities but in others the organization as a whole will act for its employees; the organization may seek to represent its beneficiaries, as may its employees, yet its beneficiaries may also find themselves co-opted to act as the organization's representatives. Still it is important to remember that when acting in the interests of its beneficiaries, NGOs and their employees are not necessarily representing them. Such is the case, for instance, when NGOs provide food aid to populations in developing countries. The provision of food is done on behalf of recipient

Figure 6.1   Model of NGO representation

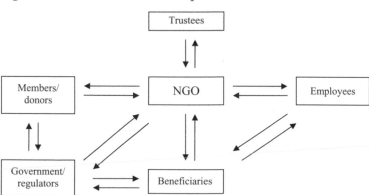

communities but not in their name. It is a charitable act, not an instance of representation.

There are, nonetheless, many cases in which an NGO's decision to act in a community's interests overlaps with the representation of those interests. While acting as advocates, lobbyists, monitors, etc., NGOs act mostly as self-appointed guardians of the interests of 'things' that cannot act for themselves (such as the environment) or as trustees of the interests of groups who are simply too big, dispersed, under-resourced or weakly coordinated to make their claims heard and considered in policy-making. Both of these gain political presence through the NGO's entrepreneurial representation, but as non-agents they cannot object by themselves to what NGOs claim in their name. So who can assert their presence in the action of NGOs, so that we can speak of representation, rather than paternalism – since as we have seen, the recipients of charitable aid are no more represented by that act than are children in receipt of food from their parents?

Objections to what NGOs do in the name of the represented can come from within NGOs themselves, especially if those with some 'stake' in their action are empowered with a greater degree of input into it, for example by being represented within its decision-making procedures. And yet most of the time the represented have no membership, voting rights or influence on the boards of the NGOs who claim to speak for them. Therefore it is also critical that their claim to represent or 'voice' the interests of their beneficiaries is subject to, and checked by, competing claims to representation, advanced by rival representatives, including other NGOs, who can give those interests a separate presence.

Recently, there have been calls for NGOs to represent entities like the environment collectively via some formal procedures of cooperation. Although it is hard to envisage how this idea could take root in the foreseeable future, for NGOs to represent the environment collectively, other accredited agents must be able to assert the environment's presence separately, by publicly objecting to what NGOs do as its self-appointed guardians. There are therefore potential costs in the pooling of resources when it comes to the representation of the relatively powerless: consensus among the representatives may lead to the diminution of representation and its replacement by paternalism, or mere 'expertise'. There may be occasions when expertise is what is needed. But experts should not assume that their expertise automatically qualifies them to act as anyone's or anything's representatives. That is a claim that must always be put to the test.

NGOs are not the only actors who have recently become politically significant forces in international relations. Other interest groups and pressure groups have demonstrated capacity to mobilize constituencies across borders, on whose behalf they try to influence decision-makers. This is the case with some traditional functional groups, for instance those representing labour (like the International Confederation of Free Trade Unions – ICFTU), which have been engaged with inter-state organizations (like the EU or the WTO) to raise the concerns of international coalitions of workers. These professional groups tend to be formally organized, membership-based associations whose activity focuses on making the views and interests of their members present to decision-makers. But there are also trans-national groups that deliberately avoid permanent, hierarchical, institutional structures. This is the case with advocacy value-based networks, such as the anti-globalization movement. Inevitably, the lack of an institutional structure comes at a cost: the assumed identity of interests or purposes among different elements of the movement is often weak and its ad hoc basis means that it is often hard to know who is speaking for whom. The legitimacy of the claims of such movements to represent their members is undermined by the difficulty of seeing how their members might object to that claim.

But there are potential gains from informality too. The flexibility and fluidity of such networked forms of organization rely on faster, cheaper and more efficient information technologies which provide new outlets for global forms of dissent. Anti-globalization activists use both cyberspace and important symbolic events, such as G8 summits, to protest and apply pressure, by giving their voice a physical presence. Their protest is often a form of objection against the perceived lack of representation offered by economic organizations, such as the World Bank, the IMF and the WTO. Hence their emphasis on visibility – on literal presence – in order to offer a contrast to the opacity of the structures of international governance. But visibility on its own is not enough to sustain durable forms of representation. It is by definition transient – it lasts as long as the spectacle lasts. Something more is needed, including clearer forms of identity, stronger lines of accountability and new means of asserting the authority of the represented to object to what is being done in their name. These aspects of representation are conventionally the province of the state which is why the advocates of non-governmental politics may be suspicious of them. But that suspicion is a weakness not a strength. Too great a reliance on visibility at the expense of more complex representative structures will leave the protestors unable to rival the representative claims of the organizations they seek to challenge.

Advocacy by public figures

Non-governmental representation is not exclusive to groups, however. It also involves individual activists, especially those who are public figures. The growing tradition of celebrity advocacy at the trans-national level has been developed both on the initiative of international organizations, such as the United Nations, with its Messengers of Peace and Goodwill Ambassadors, and by self-appointed public personalities. These include former politicians, such as Al Gore in his role as an environmental activist, and personalities from the world of entertainment, like George Clooney, Bono or Bob Geldof, acting as spokespeople of victims in Darfur or the starving in Africa.

Single activists pose us with an acute question: on what grounds can their claim to represent be justified? Obviously not on authorization: as discussed in the previous chapter, Bono has not been appointed by the poor of Africa, nor by elective officials in the poor's home countries; nor can he claim to have an independent source of authority through any professional expertise.

It is perhaps more plausible to think of Bono as represent-ing his 'constituents' by way of identification. But this too can be easily contested. Individuals, as we have seen, can identify with a social group even when they lack some of the group-defining characteristics. Since, however, *the* group-defining characteristic is, in this case, living in a condition of extreme poverty, there is, arguably, a much stronger sense of identity amongst the world's poor themselves than between them and Bono. This does not mean, however, that the poor would be better off going down the route of self-representation. Where, for instance, poor farmers represent other poor farmers hardly anyone in the wider world listens. The visibility of celebrity figures, in particular their ability to connect with people everywhere in the world, and mobilize them into action, may make them more effective spokespersons and advocates for trans-national causes than the members of the affected communities themselves. Bono cannot claim to represent the poor by dint of something they have in common. But he can argue, in a Burkean vein, that a sympathy of feelings and desires connects him to their poverty, allowing him to put himself in their shoes in his imagination, and to represent them, without actually having been chosen by them.

The absolutely poor throughout the world – those living on less than $1 a day – are too wide and dispersed a group to be able to act as a principal. Moreover, it may be that all that is necessary for their representation is that a self-appointed representative, like Bono, knows enough about their likely interests. This seems possible, as we are here speaking of the basic necessities of human life. The world poor will, arguably, have similar minimum biological needs for food, clean air, water, shelter and basic medical care that we have, and it will be in their interest if these things are provided. If we agree that their interests have a fairly objective content, a public figure may not only be able to avoid misrepresenting them but also to represent them more efficiently than the represented would do themselves. This is because public figures can speak in a language that governments and world leaders understand and find harder to ignore, given the publicity.

There are two important caveats here, however.

1. Even if the interests of the represented group are relatively uncontested, the best means of promoting them will always be open to contestation. So when Bono and

Bob Geldof praised the debt-relief package for the world's poorest countries that the G7 finance ministers announced in 2005, they faced immediate criticism, especially from African campaigners, for determining on behalf of the people in those countries whether the leaders of the G7 should be praised or blamed.

2.   Being represented by one person has at least as many disadvantages as advantages. It inevitably transforms the 'poor' into a monolithic block, obliterating their internal diversity and, more importantly, any diversity of their interests that exists alongside the uniformity of their needs. And as the represented are closely identified with one person, they gain a public face, and a strong immediate impact, but probably also one that is less sustainable over time. Public figures may help issues like genocide or global poverty enter the political agenda and mobilize people around the world. But this public often identifies less with the cause itself than with the stars that have taken it up. This means, for instance, that while viewers keep themselves up to date with Bono's doings in Africa, major structural work on the continent goes almost entirely unnoticed.

Does this mean that it would be better to represent the world's poor through more traditional representative bodies, such as their parliaments, or their appointed governments? As Clare Short, the former British Secretary of State for International Development put it at the G8 summit in July 2001: 'Who is better placed to speak on behalf of the poor, middle-class white people in the north or the elected representatives of the poor of Africa themselves?'

Short's phrasing of the question suggests the latter. But what if the world poor live, as so often happens, in failed states whose institutions are incapable of representing them in any sense, because they are non-functioning, or corrupt, or more likely both? It is true that civil society activists are overwhelmingly based in developed countries and their connection to the world poor is often fragile. But it would be seriously prejudicial to the world's poorest citizens if their governments were taken as the sole legitimate voice speaking out for them within and beyond borders. In face of the reality of failed states in developing countries, competitive (and mostly not specifically authorized) claims of activists to speak out for the world poor gain in credibility, and may well be the only way to save some of those they claim to represent from a more terrible predicament.

This co-existence of potentially multiple legitimate claims to representation at the international level has led some authors to conclude that, for the sake of fair political representation of individuals in a globalized world, we must return to the unrealized possibilities of the idea of functional representation (Kuper 2004). This means that each individual should not allow that a single representative (namely, her state) represents all her politically relevant interests internationally. She must rather entrust the representation of her different interests to different agencies (a government, an environmental NGO, a trans-national advocacy network, an international court, etc.), as well as to the indirect, often unintentional, interaction of representatives and the institutions to which they belong within the international representative system as a whole, thereby providing a series of informal checks and balances. In this no particular priority is given to those who represent us politically, i.e., to the representatives of the state who are on the same footing as any other representative.

There are obvious merits to this idea, among which is an increased emphasis on individual liberty, understood as being freed from (or in the language of republican political philosophy, being 'non-dependent' on) the arbitrary will of others. A person who permits the representation of all her interests to be placed with one and the same agent is likely to make herself vulnerable to that agent's whims. But functional representation at the international level also runs up against familiar problems which can be captured by three questions. (1) What if the different interests of a person end up being represented against one another by different functional agents? (2) What is the 'functional' role of the state if not to mediate between these different kinds of representation? (3) How is the system as a whole to be represented? For if anyone is going to be able to object to the way in which they are being represented, then we need yet another representative who does not represent the individual within the system but rather represents the individual against the system as a whole. The likelihood remains that the most plausible representatives of an individual's frustrations with the system of international governance as a whole will be national governments themselves, which may therefore be tempted to stoke these frustrations for their own benefit.

Claims to representation are never absolute: they must always prove themselves in competition with one another. When a representative acts on the explicit authorization of the represented, or at least of a majority amongst them, as is the case with democratically elected governments, then the representative has a clear head start over representatives who are self-appointed and must rely on more indirect representative links, such as trusteeship, identification, or simulation. However, in the international sphere there is some reason to think that the advantage of representatives authorized within their own electoral system is comparatively lower than in the domestic sphere.

First, at the international level, states are increasingly acting collectively, within the framework of interstate organizations (IOs). So although states have an especially strong claim to represent their citizens, the imprint of our voting – i.e., the basis of the strength of that claim – is prone to become fainter as states delegate authority from agent to agent internationally. As we shall see in the next section, every act of delegation contains a possibility of agency slack, triggered either by conflicting interests or asymmetries of information. Second, some of those people and communities who are most in need of representation live in weak, failing or failed states, whose capacity for action is minute and whose claims to representation are therefore far from credible. Third, this gives nongovernmental agencies and activists a critical role to play in global policy debates. They can provide a voice for, and advance the interests of, groups and communities who face unequal access to the international policy dialogue because of the unwillingness or the incapacity of governments to speak out for them. Every act of representation is an act of communication and at the international level that means speaking in a language the powerful will understand.

But though non-state representatives can compete with states in the domain of communication (even if it is invariably on the most powerful states' terms), the same is not true when it comes to those forms of aesthetic representation that we discussed in the previous chapter. State representation is driven by the tension that exists between the public's self-image and the image that is projected back to them by their politicians. But the globally disempowered have no real opportunity to express their view of how they are being represented. They are more like spectators who have no choice but to support whichever team happens to be playing and claiming their support. International representation by self-appointed elites, however well directed and however well intentioned, lacks the 'expressive' element that makes electoral politics so dynamic. The audience have no means of contributing to the success or failure of the performance itself.

International organizations

While all this has been going on, states have not been stand-ing still (as representative institutions par excellence, they never stand still). The sovereign status of nation-states is cur-rently undergoing significant transformation. In a highly interdependent world, states can no longer assert their sov-ereignty simply by acting independently. Instead they must find ways of taking part in collective efforts designed to solve regional and global problems within the framework of exist-ing IOs. To this end, states – while remaining the primary locus of decision-making authority – delegate some of their policy-making authority to IOs which are expected to perform various tasks on their collective behalf. In so doing, states – acting through their governments – become the principals of representative agents. But they also create the possibility for new forms of corporate representation whenever a single agent acts on their collective behalf.

The delegation of authority from principals to agents is a familiar component of modern politics. However, delegation to international agents distinguishes itself from any possible delegation to domestic agents in at least two important respects. To begin with, most delegations to IOs involve not one but two distinct aggregations of collective preferences: first, from citizens through their governments; second, from governments through IOs. As a result of this, delegation chains tend to be longer in the international than in the domestic sphere. Such 'chains' consist in the multiple stages by which the same authority is granted from one actor to another. In the simplest case, an originating principal (P1) delegates to an agent (A1) who becomes a principal (P2) who delegates to a second agent (A2). Delegation chains involving, or ending in, IOs usually start with peoples, who are represented by their governments, who are themselves represented by an agent, or multiple agents within the IO, which is in turn represented by its head. To add to the potential complications, the head of the IO may be nominated by a single government (as in the case of the World Bank, whose president is always the nominee of the United States). Here, we have representatives of IOs who may also have their authority delegated by individual agents but who nevertheless also represent the corporate body of which they are the head (see figure 6.2). The longer the chain, the greater is the potential for agency slack. This means that long chains present a problem if accountability is the issue: with every new transfer of authority, the presence of the originally represented constituency in the final representative's actions may become fainter.

Figure 6.2   IO delegation chain

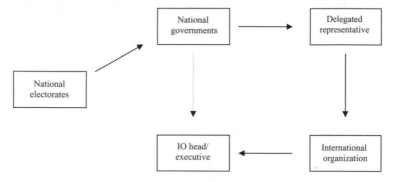

However, representation is not simply a one-way process and in its political forms it cannot be reduced to acts of delegation. The appointment of a representative creates the possibility of new kinds of accountability to new sorts of constituencies that may be created in the act of representation itself. As always, the new constituencies will have to compete with the old. So it is possible to argue both that: (1) governmental agents must remain as accountable to their domestic constituents for their intergovernmental activities as they are for their domestic ones; and (2) as members of structures of international governance, they must also take into account the interests of the other peoples affected by their decisions, 'even where these conflict with their national constituencies' (Slaughter 2004). The difficulty is knowing what incentive they would have to respond to (2), if their re-election depends almost exclusively on how (1) is played out in national politics. At the same time, it is hard to know how they should respond to (1) when decision-making in international settings is often too remote and inaccessible to admit of easy scrutiny by voters at home. Negotiating power is often so unevenly distributed in IOs that the less powerful states have hardly any say in the final outcome and only those states who are themselves global actors get to decide what is in the interest of all stakeholders. So the representatives of different principals will have different sorts of judgements to make. Yet it always remains possible that, out of a series of independent judgements, a collective judgement will emerge that allows for the representation of new international communities.

Thus there is no easy 'one size fits all' solution for improving representation within IOs. It is not even clear in many cases what improved representation – or increased 'representativeness' – would entail. These organizations vary widely in their purposes, structures and powers. This means that different IOs require different kinds of representation to meet their specific purposes. Central banks differ from development banks, executive councils from assemblies, and so on. Although the purpose of each IO must, at least partly, dictate its structure, the structure also generates its own representative dynamic and shapes the corporate personality of the institution over time. In this sense, the most significant factors in the development of representation within any institution are likely to be temporal as much as lateral. With these qualifications in mind we will pass on to a brief discussion of representation within three distinct types of international organization: the International Courts, the European Union and the United Nations.

International Courts

International Courts are usually created by treaties which are signed by states. These collectively delegate to the court authority to adjudicate certain type of disputes, by taking autonomous decisions, without an intervening interstate vote or unilateral veto. Delegation to courts has certain specificities to it, however. First, their authority is in many cases subsidiary and their jurisdiction not compulsory: for example, the International Criminal Court will investigate and prosecute crimes only if national courts are unwilling or unable to do so, not simply because it is the court most likely to give the defendant a fair trial. Second, international judges are state agents, in that they are appointed by states, though they are not state representatives. They are chosen precisely to act impartially, and promote collective goods (including the rule of international law), even against the interests of the states who have collectively delegated authority to them. Third, it is often the case that not all states delegate the same amount of authority to International Courts. For instance, since only the UN Security Council can initiate cases before the International Criminal Court, the five permanent members of the Council are the most likely sources, but also the least likely targets, of international political prosecutions.

Despite the sharp rise in the number of international judicial bodies, and of international judges acting as final arbiters on pressing issues – from responsibility for genocide, through work discrimination, to pollution and genetic manipulation – there is little public awareness of how these judges are appointed or the basis upon which their decisions are made. The common practice is that the signatory states simply select the judges. Over time states have also converged on the idea that the bench should be geographically representative, bringing together judges from the main regional groups. Accordingly, the statutes of the International Court of Justice and of the International Criminal Court establish that the judges should be representative of 'the main forms of civilization' and of 'the principal legal systems of the world'. As international legal experts chosen to represent something that cannot act for itself – i.e., the world's 'main legal systems' – the judges are asked to act as expert trustees and are forbidden from seeking or acting on instructions from any external source, particularly from within their own states (Alter 2006).

As trustees, judges bring their own source of authority to the decisions they make, according to their professional norms and best judgement. States that appoint international judicial trustees are therefore expected to step back. But judicial trusteeship will always encounter resistance from powerful states, who may seek to place themselves outside their jurisdiction (we see this in the growing US resistance to ICs). Moreover, the selection of international judicial nominees remains a highly politicized matter (Steinberg 2004). It often reflects real world power relations, or even party loyalties, at the expense of mere technical expertise. But although the appointment process is used by states to try to ensure that national positions are represented in judicial deliberations (Posner and de Figueiredo 2004), this does not necessarily mean court bias. First, at the international level, judicial decision-making involves more than one judge, so national biases can cancel themselves out; they can also be subsumed by a sense of corporate solidarity among the judges themselves. Second, because international judges are trustees, they will value their reputation as defenders of the interests of the international community, as well as the interests of those who have appointed them. Trusteeship can create its own dynamic. The claim that International Courts administer justice in the name of the world's people, and act solely in accordance with international law, clearly remains open to question but it should not be dismissed out of hand. As such, the development of these courts may reflect the dynamic potential of even relatively non-accountable forms of representation.

European Union

Concerns about a crisis of representation in the EU are long-standing (Hayward 1995). More recently, they have marked the debate surrounding the failed attempt to introduce an EU constitution and the years of constitutional and institutional wrangling leading up to the signing by EU leaders of its revised version, the EU Reform Treaty, in December 2007. For its critics, the European Union as constituted by this treaty, with its abnormally large bureaucracy and only marginally slimmed down Commission, presents a monstrous vision of what a European super-state would look like: cumbersome and unaccountable to national electorates. Reviving old fears about the creation of autocracy on a continental scale, they insist that the European space is simply too big to sustain a single representative government without sacrificing democratic accountability.

When the American Federalists faced a similar concern, their answer was that representation could release states from the constraints of geography. Gigantic states were not condemned to descend into either anarchy or despotism, as Kant predicted. Instead, a new system of representative government made popular rule possible on a previously unimaginably broad scale. The crux of the matter, in constitution making, was not geography but the quality and flexibility of the representative system.

Are we to conclude from this that the EU should follow the Madisonian model of a representative federal republic (see Siedentop 2001]? In some respects the analogy is clearly unwarranted, as it overlooks the fact that Europe comprises many well-established nation-states, operating with their own systems of checks and balances and drawing on their own cultural specificity and political identity. Nevertheless, the North American model was designed to fit any space and to allow governments to represent an entire society, notwithstanding the fact it was a society broken into many different parts, interests and classes of citizens. So if the model of one multi-level, federal republic does not suit Europe, the reason must lie, at least partly, in the quality of representation on offer, rather than in the impossibility of Europe being represented in this way. The difficulty of achieving European-wide political representation is a contingent not an absolute fact: it means simply that there are better models of representation on offer, not that Europe itself is an 'unrepresentable' entity. Nor should we assume that a Madisonian representative politics must be as Madison himself envisaged it. Madison and the other Founding Fathers were deeply sceptical about the role of political parties in holding a representative system together; they thought parties were more likely to pull it apart. But political parties have been essential in coupling together representation and democracy in larger states, particularly at times of national crisis, not least in the US. Similarly, it is hard to imagine a sustainable European politics in the absence of Europe-wide political parties, capable of offering the European electorate some competing visions of their own representation. Only competition of this kind can offer a unifying vehicle for the many, often competing, ambitions of the various European peoples, including their simultaneous desire to have a share in power and to be left alone (Siedentop 2001). But it is hard to envision how a genuinely European politics can emerge from the parties we currently have.

The only direct election of IO representatives with authority to take binding decisions is within the EU. However, elections to the European Parliament are carried on a national basis and fought by national parties with overwhelmingly national agendas. When MEPs reach Strasbourg they sit in groups that purport to represent shared political beliefs. But these groups fall short of European-wide parties, willing to compete to represent Europe as a whole. How – one might ask – can such parties emerge in the face of the seeming indifference national European electorates display to the idea that they are all in this together? Lying behind this question is often a sense that Europe can only be represented as a whole if there is something whole to represent: a unity of peoples, a genuine demos.

However, as Hobbes stressed, we are wrong to assume that such unity must exist prior to, and independently of, the process of representation. European peoples do not, and will not, naturally exist as a unity which is already present to itself. This unity will need to be made present to them by their representatives. And their representatives will need an incentive to offer them such a vision. In electoral politics, the incentive is power: parties must be convinced there is a political prize worth fighting for, a prize they have some chance of winning. At the moment, the prize of power within the electoral structures of the EU is not sufficient for this. The incentive would be higher if the representatives of the EU had something to unify against. Historically, war has played a central role in cementing durable political relationships of representation, as in the US, where the creation of the representative republic coincided with a series of military conflicts, first for independence, then for expansion, and finally a civil war that set two competing visions of political representation against each other. For now, the representatives of Europe lack a similarly tangible enemy to confront.

This shows the danger of drawing historical analogies. It would be absurd to think that what Europe needs for the sake of its own representation as a unified whole is a war, least of all a civil war. Indeed, if the price of seeking to represent Europe as a whole were the prospect of civil war, then that would seem to be a good reason for avoiding projects of European-wide political representation. In the meantime, European governments have agreed on an EU Reform Treaty that seems to be trying to appropriate the central lesson of the Hobbesian model of representation – that centralized power can create unity rather than depend on it – but to do so by stealth. Yet unlike Hobbes's *Leviathan*, Europe as currently constituted is a three-headed, not a one-headed, monster: each of its three main institutions – Council, Commission and Foreign Policy – has presidential functions and a head of its own. Hobbes feared that a beast like this would fall apart and the state collapse into anarchy. That will not happen to the EU, since the nation-states, each a solid Hobbesian creation in its own right, will be there to pick up the pieces.

There are perhaps two lessons here. The first is that representation is not something that is easy to achieve by stealth – it must be, in Hobbes's terms, 'legible', or as later theorists might put it, visible. Visibility on its own is not enough either but, without any clear projection of what it is that is being represented, no representative politics will endure. Second, while it is absurd to wish some crisis on the EU that requires it to project a vision of itself as a coherent political order, such a crisis is possible in a world that remains dangerous and unpredictable. If it comes, the representative bodies of the EU will have an incentive to try to produce a compelling vision of what it is, and who it is, they are ultimately for.

United Nations

Judging by its Charter, the United Nations (UN) is the only all-embracing site for the political representation of peoples around the world. Charged with ensuring global peace and security, as well as the worldwide enforcement of human rights, the United Nations appears to be one of the strongest contenders for the representation of the most vital interests of a global public. But with its massive dependency on governments and their resources, it is clear that the UN as it currently operates is primarily a site for the representation of nation-states through their appointed delegates.

Does it have to be this way? Could the UN's principal organs, the Security Council and the General Assembly, ever be plausible bodies for global political representation? What reforms of representative institutions within the UN, if any, could help them fulfil that goal?

To answer these questions, we need to address the vexed issue of UN membership: who is and who should be represented in this institution of global governance? The UN, like most IOs, works through a chain of delegation whose most important link is between sovereign states and the organs of the United Nations. This means that the selection and removal of delegates within the main bodies of the UN belongs exclusively to states and their governments. (The UN Charter begins with the phrase 'We the people', but it is worth remembering that this came in place of the original 'The high contracting parties [i.e., the states]'.) In addition, besides being an organization constituted by states, the UN is also an organization dominated by the select group of permanent members of its executive body: the Security Council.

As a world organization, the United Nations abides by the principle of full inclusiveness. This means it is open to all states that commit themselves to the letter of the UN Charter and its Declarations, irrespective of whether they accord to these principles in practice. Against the background of these principles, however, the formal equality of all members exists in tension with their varying levels of legitimation which is necessarily higher in liberal-democratic countries than in their semi-authoritarian and authoritarian counterparts. The tension reaches an ironic climax when the representative of a country like Libya is elected to the chair of the Human Rights Commission.

Cases like this give rise to the claim that the United Nations cannot aspire to be a body representing the interests of peoples worldwide if a substantial number of its member states are largely illiberal and undemocratic. This is because the publics at the start of delegation chains in non-democratic countries are so narrowly drawn, and their outlets for objection so limited, that it makes little or no sense to maintain that the votes of their delegates within the UN represent the views or the interests of their peoples. So if the first link in the delegation chain is undemocratic, other chains will be necessarily corrupted.

This argument opens up two possible ways of thinking about what theories of representation at the international level should amount to. For some, representation must be constructed according to certain normative criteria external to it (i.e., in the language of democracy) if it is to be legitimate at all. In practice, this means that political representation, strictly speaking, depends on democratic institutions (such as free elections) in order to be properly grounded. When this legitimacy claim is taken into account in considering representation within IOs, there are two alternatives: (1) membership within the IO should be restricted to liberal democracies (as is currently the case with the EU); (2) membership should remain open to all but the state's voting power within the IO will be reduced if it does not have a fully functioning democratic system at home.

This view contrasts with that of those who think representation is always in service to some particular purpose or function and should simply be assessed by reference to that, not least because representation, per se, is not a democratic concept at all (Rehfeld 2006). So if efficiency is the main purpose to be pursued by an institution, then the model of representation it must follow will be different than if its purpose is democratic legitimacy.

In the case of core UN organs, such as the Security Council and the General Assembly, their representative structure must be considered in terms of, first, what they are for and, second, what type of composition and decision procedures best suit their different functions.

As the custodian of the collective security interests of the international community, the Security Council was established as a body where the representation of diversity could be trumped by representation as decision-making. This meant that the actors represented in the Security Council were to be: (1) few in number and relatively homogeneous; (2) capable of supporting UN activities, primarily through their monopoly of force. Hence the original Council's composition transplanted the global power structure of 1945: the state actors victorious in the war became its permanent members and were given a greater say in its decisions. But they were also given a veto power which was designed to bind them to any decisions taken but which makes the reaching of collective decisions much more difficult.

This has enormous consequences in terms of delegation of authority to and within the UN. Non-members of the Council delegate authority to the Council to make binding decisions regarding collective security on their behalf. The same happens with the ten states that are elected from amongst all states represented in the UN as non-permanent members of the Security Council (according to quotas based on geographical criteria to ensure parity between continents), since the veto-wielding permanent members can bind them to decisions over and above their objections. But the five permanent members of the Security Council have only granted authority to the Council on condition that they are not bound by it against their will. Their power to veto any Council decision means that no binding decision can be adopted without their agreement. The delegates of the permanent members represent their principals in ways that trump the ability of the Council to represent all its members as a whole.

The realities of power relations as they existed in 1945 have long since been superseded. Yet the composition of the Security Council remains unchanged. A change in the power relationships within the Security Council, together with strong limitations on veto rights, would be necessary if the Council were to become the locus of a more corporate form of representation. But an expansion of membership, aiming at both the representation of the new global structure of power and of greater geographic diversity, would be counterproductive if diversity gets in the way of effective decision-making. Proposals for widening representation on the Security Council, with up to twenty-four members recruited from amongst states, interstate and non-state actors, especially if combined with veto powers, tend to ignore a critical fact: inclusion is traded off for efficiency (Kuper 2004).

If representation within the Security Council, with its necessary emphasis on action, must always remain somehow 'selective', could the General Assembly (GA) ever be a plausible body for global representation? Various alternative models for improving representation within the GA have been advanced in recent years. They tend to have one thing in common: they want the GA to better reflect the diversity of the wider international community by increasing its size and the internal diversity of its composition.

For some, this implies the establishment of a 'second chamber' alongside the GA which could work as a parliament of world citizens, representing territorial actors other than states. This might then gradually be superseded by a 'global parliament', possibly constituted through direct global elections on the basis of territorial constituencies (Held 1998). Others would prefer it if the GA represented both governments and their oppositions, with at least one of the delegates of each country being directly elected (Archibugi 1998). A third group recommends the multiplication of deliberative bodies, each guaranteeing the representation of different 'constituencies': diverse individuals chosen from all over the world, as well as governments, corporations, local authorities and NGOs. The directly elected people's assembly would be the UN's sovereign body, responsible for making laws, budgets and appointments; state governments would provide its executive power (Galtung 2000). Finally, there are those who wish to shape the GA according to the imperatives of functional representation: individuals must have representatives who speak for them in accordance with the different social groups to which they belong. Any single individual would have multiple different representatives at the global level, all of which would combine to produce a more systematic responsiveness to the interests and judgements of the global public (Kuper 2004).

None of these proposals worries much about gigantism, or whether greater inclusiveness will be inefficient in assuring legitimacy. The baroque institutional architectures they put forward are, nonetheless, a potential recipe for paralysis, or perhaps for rule by a coalition of illiberal states, substituting for the current 'great powers', or even for rule by one parliamentary hegemon – a single power or a minority of powerful states, capable of offering a way out of paralysis and bringing smaller states into compliance. Inclusion does not always mean democratization because enhanced representation can pull in many different directions. An increase in the number of groups who are 'seen' in the UN may go along with a decrease in the number who are actually heard.

World government

The answer to the question of whether the General Assembly can ever be a plausible body for global representation cannot simply be decided by whether it is possible to speak for the world public in all its internal diversity. For the question cannot be considered in the abstract. Representation is always competitive in that claims to representation depend on whether they can trump competing claims to represent. And it is very hard to see how an enlarged world parliamentary assembly, granting equal voting powers to self-appointed and elected representatives, could win such a contest either with national states, regional alliances or networks of interest groups.

As it stands, the United Nations is not a world government but a forum for the world's sovereign states to debate issues of global importance and determine collective courses of action. But the campaign for a world federalist government, founded upon a directly elected world parliamentary assembly, is once again gathering pace (Monbiot 2003). Are there any circumstances in which the idea of all humankind united under, and represented by, one common political authority would be either feasible or desirable?

As Hobbes said, almost anything can be represented ('there are few things that are uncapable of being represented by Fiction') but, as he was also very aware, it all depends on the credibility of the fiction and on the reasons people have for believing in it. So although almost *any*thing, and *any*where, can be represented, *every*thing and *every*where cannot. A world state makes a far-fetched object of representation because states need something to contrast themselves with. A world community of citizens, even if generating a democratically elected representative body, would lack any convincing picture of itself to represent.

In all probability, global representation would have to fall back on the language of human rights. These rights can generate international legal procedures and stronger structures of impartial adjudication between rival sovereign claims. Their violation at one place is increasingly capable of being felt at all others by a widening mechanism of sympathy driven by the spread of information technology. They can even produce a negative consensus, founded on a common outrage at human rights violations, given cross-culturally recognized negative duties of refraining from crimes against humanity and wars of aggression. What they cannot provide is that thicker sense of identity, or the sort of positive solidarity, which political parties think worth constructing and fighting for.

An idea as abstract as that of a parliament of world citizens, resting on trans-national constituencies of millions of individuals and inhabited by representatives representing populations loosely bound together by a common outrage at human rights violations, faces immediate charges of naivety and utopianism. And reasonably so: in what would the democratic competition for seats in such a world parliament consist? Is there room for competition at all within such a tame negative consensus? Moreover, as the distance between represented and representative widens, accountability becomes a pressing problem. The spectre of appallingly low voter turnouts, complete lack of voter recognition of their global representatives, scanty knowledge of what they propose to do, and why, would be haunting. And yet the concept of representation has in the past stretched the limits of political imagination. Three major revolutions – in England, America and France – were mother to three distinct types of modern representative government. So the question remains whether there are any circumstances in which global representation might be realizable. Do we have enough time and/or the imaginative resources to give it the legitimacy it needs, without the kind of crises that it would be needed to confront, namely a global environmental catastrophe?

Epilogue: Representing the Future?

So, can representative politics meet the challenges that the world is likely to face in the future? Certainly, one common complaint made against the dominant form of representative politics in the modern world – politics centred on the state and organized around elections, political parties and public opinion – concerns its limited time horizons. The structures of democratic representation often appear to encourage politicians to worry about their imminent fate at the polls at the expense of longer-term considerations. A criticism of this kind lies behind many of the attempts to think about representation beyond the nation-state described in the previous chapter.

But it is important to recognize that the short-termism of electoral politics at the national level is also a part of its strength because of its ability to respond to shifts in the public mood. Even if politicians cannot be instructed by the public to do as the public would like, the public can at least get rid of them if they do not like what the politicians do. Although this will usually be a retrospective judgement, based on the failure of politicians to live up to expectations, it provides a motivation for politicians to look forward, in order to anticipate how the public might react to their behaviour in the future (not least, it ought to encourage politicians not to make promises they cannot keep) (Manin 1997). This process is increasingly supplemented by the detailed ongoing sampling of public opinion, which allows politicians to read the public mood in relation to their present or future plans. None of this means that anyone is thinking very long term and the resulting politics is likely to be more reactive than pro-active. But it does mean that within its short time horizons, representative politics is able to look forward as well as back.

However, in this book we have argued that representation is an open-ended concept that is able to accommodate a wide range of different political visions, including long- as well as short-term political thinking. Certainly representation is a more open-ended concept than democracy, which is inevitably tied to the will of the majority (and this suggests that if our current politics is dynamic only within short-term horizons, it is because it is a democratic form of representation, rather than because it is the representative form of democracy). The history of representation also offers evidence of its potential as a transformative concept, able to provide the vehicle for dramatic, even revolutionary, political change. There is no reason to suppose, therefore, that representative politics *cannot* incorporate long-term and wide-ranging thinking about the problems the world currently faces.

But it is also the case that where the concept of representation has proved its worth as a mechanism for managing significant change, this has been in circumstances of political crisis and most often of war (both civil and international). It is at times of crisis that the concept of representation has shown its flexibility as a political tool by providing a conceptual means for the reordering of politics, transcending the constraints of sectional or local prejudices and reconciling the apparently irreconcilable interests and perspectives of the inhabitants of a single political space.

But what about dealing with crises before they arise or heading them off before they become too serious? We live in a world with problems that may well require pre-emptive thinking and that threaten not merely political crises but potential catastrophe (Rees 2003). These problems include global warming, resource depletion (oil, food, water, clean air), the threat of terrorism and the possibility of global pandemics. Thinking about these issues involves considering the

long-term future consequences of our present actions and that
in turn may require that we give the future a greater presence
in our present-oriented politics. We have emphasized more
than once in this book that anything can be represented (even
though not everything can be represented at the same time).
So how might it be possible to represent the future?

It is necessary to distinguish between two different kinds
of answer to this question, one of which can be characterized
as 'negative' and the other as 'positive'. A negative approach
to the problem of future representation emphasizes the importance of making sure that future generations are not unthink-
ingly implicated in the decisions we take. In other words,
we should not assume that future generations are automatically represented in our decisions, which means that we
must not build into our own decisions assumptions about
their enduring quality. The practical implication would be
that future generations are not bound by our decisions. This
would make it harder for us to exploit the inability of future
generations to express their own preferences by burdening
them with the consequences of our own recklessness. For
example, it would mean that we could not borrow large
sums in the present on the assumption that these debts would
be paid off in the future because it would be open to future
generations to repudiate our debts. This is in fact what sometimes happens under systems of democratic representation
where representatives justify repudiation on the grounds that
those whom they represent now cannot afford the obligations
incurred by earlier generations (see, for example, the recent
debt crisis in Argentina). The short time horizons of representative politics can work both ways: as well as encouraging present generations to impose burdens on the future, it
also allows them to refuse the burdens imposed on them
by the past.

The difficulty with this negative conception is that it presupposes a break between the present and the future which
makes it hard to see how the interests of the present and the
future might be made to join up. In that respect, it looks like
the enemy of long-term thinking. Moreover, though the aim
is to ensure that current generations do not take future
generations for granted, the absence of joined-up thinking

may serve to make the burdens of each greater. Take the example of public debt. If it is known that the repayment of long-term debt is subject to the discretion of future representatives, that would simply make it harder to borrow in the present (when it comes to debt, the shorter the time horizons, the higher the interest). Equally, the fact that it is possible to repudiate debt that was contracted by previous generations does not make the job of present representatives any easier – any act of repudiation also makes it much harder (and more expensive) to borrow money in the immediate future. So the consequences of earlier recklessness will still be felt. Public debt is a good example of an issue where stability and security depend on present generations being able to bind future generations (see Ferguson 2001). The same is almost certainly true of environmental questions where we need some confidence that any decisions we take to restrict the depletion of natural resources will hold not just for ourselves but for those who are to follow us. Of course, that still leaves open the question of whether the distribution of burdens will be a fair one. If high levels of indebtedness in the present are a means of avoiding difficult decisions about taxation and welfare provision, then the burden of these decisions will be transferred to the future along with the debts. But what that suggests is that something more than a negative conception of future representation is required. Instead, we need some positive means of taking account of the interests of future generations in the decisions we take in the present.

A positive conception of future representation is one that seeks to find or appoint representatives of future generations, able to speak up and speak out for the interests of those who cannot speak for themselves. Inevitably, this will not be representation founded on a standard principal–agent model, where this is understood to entail the authorization or instruction of the representatives by those being represented. Future generations need representation precisely because they cannot instruct anyone to act for them and therefore risk being left out of decision-making that may vitally affect their interests. So this will invariably entail representation on something like a trusteeship model, whereby representatives are appointed to look after the interests of those who would otherwise be incapacitated by their inability to act for themselves.

As we saw in chapter 3, trusteeship emerged as a legal device primarily in order to protect the property and other interests of future generations, including the unborn, and many legal trusts are still organized on that basis today. But as well as overlapping with the trustee model, the political representation of future generations is liable to get mixed up with tenuous forms of identity politics. When it comes to knowing *who* should speak for the future, we may want to turn to people who can somehow identify with what future generations would wish us to do. But who is going to have this special insight? The young, who might have a more tangible conception of the future, given the greater probability that they will have to inhabit it? The old, who have more experience of how things can pan out in the long term? Or, alternatively, those who have a particular stake in certain issues with long-term ramifications, such as professional ecologists, environmental campaigners or the champions of civil liberties? The fact that it might just be plausible to make a claim for any of these different groups shows how difficult it will be to find a form of identity politics here that is likely to stick.

In the absence of anyone with a special claim to know how future generations might think, a more significant question is likely to be how such representatives will be appointed and how they are going to compare to – and just as importantly, compete with – the representatives of more conventional constituencies. One possible answer is to envisage future generations as though they were just another constituency, to be represented within the political process alongside everyone else. This could, for example, be achieved by a system of proportional representation that set aside a quota of representatives specifically empowered to speak on behalf of the unborn. One possible advantage of such a scheme would be that it appears to take the representation of the future seriously by refusing to distinguish between the interests of those who can and those who cannot actually vote. But the obvious disadvantage is that it would do nothing to alter the fact that only one set of representatives under such a scheme would be answerable to constituents who can actually vote and thereby dissent from what is being done on their behalf. Given the integral role that dissent plays in any form of political representation, it is hard to see how treating future generations as though they were no different from any other constituency could avoid marginalizing them, since future generations would be the only ones who could never actually say 'no' to what is being done in their name. Representatives who have to stand for election are usually more constrained than those who don't. But the fact that they are constrained also makes it much easier for them to refuse to back down. In the dynamic of representative politics, the present is always likely to win out over the future if the future has to compete with the present on equal terms.

So the representatives of the future are likely to need some kind of special protection under any competitive system of government. At this point, one might ask why the unborn need the kind of special protection that is not available to other groups of people who lack the ability to speak for themselves, such as young children (Kavka and Warren 1983). Why do children not have their own representatives as well? Perhaps the clearest answer is that they already do, in the form of all those representatives, and all those voters, who have children and take children's interests into account when they decide how to act. As Kavka and Warren put it: 'Existing children have this one huge advantage over future generations, especially distant generations: we care much more *about* the former. We see Susie and Johnny; we touch them . . . Our imaginations usually fail to conjure up the details of future persons, and so we generally fail to identify with them and their interests' (ibid.: 27). The implication of this is that future generations, especially somewhat distant ones, have a particular need for special representatives because the representative system is unlikely to conjure up a convincing picture of their interests on its own, without some additional help.

The Israeli parliament is one of the first to have tried to implement a scheme that leaves open a specified place for the representation of future generations in its decisions, by giving future generations a representative with distinctive rights and responsibilities within the legislative process. Many other systems of government have branches of the executive tasked with long-term thinking (in most cases, these are known as offices of 'sustainable development'). What makes the Israeli experiment so distinctive is its allocation of a role for representation of the future in the drafting of legislation. Since 2001 the Knesset has had a Commission for Future Generations whose head, a Commissioner appointed by the Speaker of the parliament, must be consulted on every piece of legislation before it can be passed into law. The comments or recommendations of the Commissioner must be included as explanatory notes on every bill before its second and third readings. In addition, the Commissioner is able to request information from any branch of government, and 'from time to time and at his own discretion, prepare reports with recommendations on issues that have a special interest for future generations' ('Commission for Future Generations', 6). The areas of interest covered by the Commission include the environment, health, natural resources, pensions, demography and quality of life.

It is much too early to know how much difference, if any, such a Commissioner might make to Israeli politics (indeed, until some future generations get an opportunity to judge how well their interests have been represented, the success of this project will have to remain an open question). But what does seem clear is that the holder of this office is likely be acting in a primarily reactive role, raising issues in response to pieces of legislation that appear to ignore long-term considerations, rather than initiating pieces of legislation that prioritize the future over the present. It is true that the Commissioner is empowered to convene a public council of scientists, intellectuals, clergy and others to discuss and raise issues of long-term significance. But one does not have to be unduly sceptical about the political efficacy of such bodies, nor about the sort of functional representation that they embrace, to wonder what real impact such a body might have. Any form of political representation, as we have emphasized throughout this book, must set its claims not simply against non-representation but against rival forms of representation, offering alternative modes of political expression to the relevant constituency. Giving the future a presence by airing various issues is not enough. The future has to have a presence that can compete with the representation of the present itself. This will be hard to achieve in any reasonably competitive system of representative government (and Israeli politics is nothing if not competitive).

It might be argued that the problem here is the direct contrast between present and future and between the representation of people who actually exist and the representation of people who do not exist but merely might. One way round this is to get away from thinking about the future in terms of the people who will inhabit it and instead to look towards the representation of the entities that link the present to the future, such as the environment or even the planet itself. The concept of trusteeship certainly allows for the representation of such abstractions as the environment, just as it allows for the representation of all sorts of impersonal or non-human entities (ranging from wildlife reserves to endangered species). In depersonalizing the interests being represented, trusteeship invites claims to speak objectively on their behalf by scientific spokespersons, such as biologists and ecologists. However, these epistemic claims do not rule out contestability. More than the particular scientific claims as such, what remains open to question is which claims are normatively relevant to the representation of the environment – those concerning the welfare of individuals or those concerning the functioning of ecosystems. Although the expectation is that in most cases the good of individuals and the good of ecosystems will be positively related, they will sometimes come apart – as for example when measures to combat global warming threaten the economic growth of developing countries – and the decision of what to do then lies at the centre of politics. Another connected difficulty with the representation of the environment, or the planet, is that the represented entity is so general it may be hard to specify what its distinctive interests are. This is a different problem from the all-inclusive indeterminacy of a global state because at least it would be possible to contrast the long-term and encompassing interests of the planet with the short-term and partial interests of some of those who are despoiling it.

To put it bluntly, a trustee whose job it was to speak up for the environment in a parliamentary setting would probably not have much difficulty in finding other representatives to argue against.

The real difficulty lies with the idea of trusteeship itself. Trusteeship depends on two particular conditions if it is to operate successfully. First, there needs to be a clear understanding of who has the right to appoint trustees and this will usually be someone with a particular claim over the incapable person or thing to be represented (as with parents and their children or the benefactors of charitable trusts and their money). Second, those who appoint the trustees then need to be willing to stand back and allow the trustees discretion to exercise their own judgement – above all, those who authorize trusts need to resist the temptation to keep interfering. Both of these conditions are hard to meet when it comes to the political representation of the planet. The universality of the entity to be represented makes it hard for anyone to assert a particular claim over its representation. Those who do have particular claims – such as environmental organizations and other bodies with an established track record of taking the interests of the planet seriously – are not themselves universal but particular organizations which means they will always be suspected not just of particularity but also, crucially, of partiality. Meanwhile, the organizations with the real power to appoint trustees – states – are also the ones that are least likely to stand back and allow those trustees the discretion they need. It is not by chance that trusteeship is usually invoked as a political option in the case of weak states (see, for example, Hertz 2004). This is precisely because weak states lack the power to intervene. But strong states, which are the ones that will be needed to back up the terms of any global trust, are the ones it will be the hardest to persuade not to interfere.

In a sense, we are back here with the basic outline, and basic difficulties, of the Hobbesian conception of representation that we encountered in the first chapter of this book. For Hobbes, representation is what makes the state possible but the state is also what makes representation possible. The concept of representation allows for the representation of all sorts of incapable entities – 'a Bridge, an Hospital, a

Church', as Hobbes says, so why not also a planet? The problem is that these fictions only survive and endure if they have the power of the state to reinforce their representation and to give protection to their representatives. We are therefore still stuck with the difficulty of getting beyond a Hobbesian conception of representation. A global state, with the power to tackle global problems in its own right, remains a distant and deeply uncertain prospect. But all other forms of representation will have to rely for their enduring hold on our politics, and on our imaginations, on the power of the state, which remains the definitive representative institution and is unlikely to give up its power easily, or without a struggle.

It may be that some kind of global crisis is around the corner which will require the coordination of state activities into wider and more powerful representative bodies with genuine global reach. But the kinds of crises that might produce these outcomes are neither something that anyone should wish for nor expect to be able to manage with any confidence. Crises, by definition, produce unpredictable results. Nor should we assume that if and when the moment comes for global political action that the resulting politics will be democratic. It is true that representation and democracy have become inextricably bound together in the politics of the state but, as this book has tried to show, that process took time to mature and was by no means an inevitable result of the logic of representation. The logic of representation allows for a wide variety of different political outcomes. Moreover, time may be one of the resources we currently lack.

So perhaps there are just two things we can say with confidence, as we reach the end of this book. First, whatever solutions are to be found to the problems the world currently faces, they will have to involve representation in some form or other since there is no plausible form of politics in the modern world that can eschew the concept of representation altogether. We cannot do without representation if we are to assert our presence, and shape our environment, collectively. Second, given the difficulties (of authorization, accountability, identity, legitimacy and presence) involved in representing 'the future' or 'the planet' in ways that can compete with the representative politics of the state, we cannot rely on some alternative model of representation to come to our rescue. If global problems are to have realistic solutions, it will depend on the representative politics we are familiar with in the present. And that means – judging by how representative politics has come to evolve since the time of Hobbes – it will depend not on the representation of future generations, or the children, or the planet. It will depend on the representation of *us*.

References

Authors' names appear in square brackets when the texts in question were published anonymously, but the authorship has since been established beyond doubt.

Adamczick-Gerteis (ed.) (1997). 'Annex: The Pontigano Conference on Aspects of UN Reform: Discussion', in *Documents on United Nations Reform*. Aldershot: Dartmouth, pp. 560–3.

Alcoff, Linda (1995). 'The Problem of Speaking for Others', in *Who Can Speak*, ed. Judith Rood and Robyn Wiegman. Chicago: University of Illinois Press, pp. 97–119.

Alter, Karen (2006). 'Delegation to International Courts and the Limits of Re-contracting Political Power', in *Delegation and Agency in International Organizations*, ed. D. Hawkins, D. A. Lake, D. Nielson and M. J. Tierney. Cambridge: Cambridge University Press, pp. 312–38.

Ankersmit, F. R. (1997). *Aesthetic Politics: Political Philosophy Beyond Fact and Value*. Stanford, Calif.: Stanford University Press.

Ankersmit, F. R. (2002). *Political Representation*. Stanford, Calif.: Stanford University Press.

Anon. (1643). *Plain Dealing with England*. London.

Archibugi, D. (1998). 'Principles of Cosmopolitan Democracy', in *Re-imagining Political Community: Studies in Cosmopolitan Democracy*, ed. D. Archibugi, D. Held and M. Kohler. Stanford, Calif.: Stanford University Press, pp. 198–228.

Arnold, G. (1997). *World Government by Stealth: The Future of the United Nations*. London: Macmillan.

Barber, Benjamin (1989). *Strong Democracy: Participatory Politics for a New Age*. Berkeley: University of California Press.

Beer, Samuel (1965). *British Politics in a Collectivist Age*. New York: Knopf.

Beitz, C. (1983). 'Cosmopolitan Ideals and National Sentiment', *Journal of Philosophy* 80: 10591–600.

Beitz, C. (1994). 'Cosmopolitan Liberalism and the State System', in *Political Restructuring in Europe: Ethical Perspectives*, ed. C. Brown. London and New York: Routledge, pp. 123–36.

Bentham, Jeremy (2002). *Rights, Representation and Reform. Nonsense upon Stilts and Other Writings on the French Revolution*, ed. Philip Schofield et al. Oxford: Clarendon Press.

Bianco, W. T. (1994). *Trust: Representatives and Constituents*. Ann Arbor: University of Michigan Press.

Brand, P. (2004). 'Petitions and Parliament in the Reign of Edward I', in *Parchment and People: Parliament in the Middle Ages*, ed. L. Clark, *Parliamentary History* 23/1: 14–38.

Brennan, Geoffrey and Hamlin, Alan (1999). 'On Political Representation', *British Journal of Political Science* 29: 109–27.

Brown, B. (1998). 'Summary: A Mid-Life Crisis for the UN at Fifty', in *Past Imperfect, Future Uncertain: The United Nations at Fifty*. Basingstoke: Macmillan, pp. 243–62.

Brown, Louise F. (1939). 'Ideas of Representation from Elizabeth to Charles II', *Journal of Modern History* 21: 23–40.

Brown, L. N. and T. Kennedy (2000). *The Court of Justice of the European Communities*, 5th edn. London: Sweet and Maxwell.

Brown, Mark B. (2006). 'Survey Article: Citizen Panels and the Concept of Representation', *The Journal of Political Philosophy* 14/2: 203–25.

Brutus ([1787–8] 1985). 'Essays of Brutus', in *The Complete Anti-Federalist Papers*, ed. Herbert J. Storing and Murray Dry. 7 vols, Chicago, Ill.: University of Chicago Press, II, pp. 358–452.

Burke, Edmund ([1774] 1854–6). 'Speech to the Electors of Bristol', in *The Works of the Right Honourable Edmund Burke*. London: Henry G. Bohn, I, pp. 446–8.

Burke, Edmund ([1790] 1987). *Reflections on the Revolution in France*, ed. J. G. A. Pocock. Indianapolis: Hackett Publishing Company.

Burke, Edmund ([1757] 1990). *A Philosophical Enquiry into the Origin of our Ideas of the Sublime and the Beautiful*, ed. Adam Phillips. Oxford: Oxford University Press.

Burke, Edmund (1993). *Pre-Revolutionary Writings*, ed. Ian Harris. Cambridge: Cambridge University Press.

Burns, J. H. and Izbicki, Thomas (eds) (1998). *Conciliarism and Papalism*. Cambridge: Cambridge University Press.

Cameron, Charles, Epstein, David and O'Halloran, Sharyn (1996). 'Do Majority–Minority Districts Maximize Substantive Black Representation in Congress?', *American Political Science Review* 90/4: 794–812.

Canning, J. P. (1983). 'Ideas of the State in the Thirteenth and Fourteenth Century Commentators on the Roman Law', *Transactions of the Royal Historical Society*, 5th series 33: 1–27.

Childers, E. and B. Urquhart (1994). 'Renewing the United Nations System', in *Reforming the United Nations: New Initiatives and Past Efforts*, ed. J. Muller, 3 vols. The Hague: Kluwer Law International, III, pp. 38/1–209.

Cicero ([44BC] 1913). *De officiis (On duties)*, trans. Walter Miller. Cambridge, Mass.: Harvard University Press.

Cicero ([55BC] 1942). *De Oratore (On the Orator)*, trans. H. Rackham, 2 vols. Cambridge, Mass.: Harvard University Press, I.

Clarke, M. V. (1936). *Medieval Representation and Consent*. London: Longmans, Green and Co.

Cole, G. D. H. (1920). *Essays in Social Theory*. London: Macmillan.

'Commission for Future Generations' (2007). The Knesset/Israeli Parliament <www.knesset.gov.il/sponsorship/future/eng/overview. pdf>, accessed 16/11/07.

Conover, Pamela Johnston (1988). 'The Role of Social Groups in Political Thinking', *British Journal of Political Science* 18/1: 51–76.

Constant, Benjamin ([1815 and 1819] 1988). 'Principles of Politics Applicable to All Representative Governments' and 'The Liberty of the Ancients Compared with that of the Moderns', in *Constant: Political Writings*, ed. B. Fontana. Cambridge: Cambridge University Press, pp. 170–328.

Coote, A. and J. Lenahan (1997). *Citizens' Juries: Theory into Practice*. London: Institute for Public Policy Research.

Crosby, Ned (1996). 'Citizen Juries: One Solution for Difficult Environmental Problems', in *Fairness and Competence in Citizen Participation*, ed. Ortwin Renn et al., Norwell, MA: Kluwer Academic Publishers, pp. 157–74.

Dahl, Robert (1971). *Polyarchy: Participation and Opposition*. New Haven, Conn.: Yale University Press.

Dahl, Robert (1991). *Democracy and its Critics*. New Haven, Conn.: Yale University Press.

Davies, R. G. and J. H. Denton (eds) (1981). *The English Parliament in the Middle Ages*. Manchester: Manchester University Press.

D'Ewes, Sir Simonds (1682). *The Journals of All the Parliaments during the Reign of Queen Elizabeth*. London.

[Digges, Dudley] (1642). *An Answer to a Printed Book*, Oxford.

Digges, Dudley (1643). *The Unlawfulnesse of Subjects Taking up Armes against their Sovereigne, in what case soever*, Oxford.

Dobson, Andrew (1996). 'Representative Democracy and the Environment', in *Democracy and the Environment*, ed. W. Lafferty and J. Meadowcraft. Cheltenham: Edward Elgar, pp. 124–39.

Dovi, Suzanne (2002). 'Preferable Descriptive Representatives: Will Just Any Woman, Black or Latino Do?', *American Political Science Review* 96/4: 729–43.

Dunn, John (1984). 'The Concept of "Trust" in the Politics of John Locke', in *Philosophy in History*, ed. R. Rorty, J. B. Schneewind and Quentin Skinner. Cambridge: Cambridge University Press, pp. 279–301.

Dunn, John (1999). 'Situating Democratic Political Accountability', in *Democracy, Accountability, and Representation*, ed. A. Przeworski, S. Strokes, and B. Manin. Cambridge: Cambridge University Press, pp. 329–44.

Eckersley, Robyn (2000). 'Deliberative Democracy, Ecological Representation and Risk', in *Democratic Innovation: Deliberation, Representation and Association*, ed. Michael Saward. London: Routledge, pp. 117–32.

Edwards, J. G. (1970). 'The Plena Potestas of English Parliamentary Representatives', in *Historical Studies of the English Parliament*, ed. E. B. Fryde and E. Miller, 2 vols. Cambridge: Cambridge University Press, I, pp. 136–49.

Elton, G. R. (1969). *'The Body of the Whole Realm': Parliament and Representation in Medieval and Tudor England*. Virginia: Virginia University Press.

Faggioli, Massimo and Melloni, Alberto (eds.) (2006). *Repraesentatio: Mapping a Keyword for Churches and Governance*. Berlin: PLIT Verlag.

Fassbender, B. (1998). *UN Security Council Reform and the Right of Veto: A Constitutional Perspective*. The Hague: Kluwer International.

Faulk, R. (2000). 'On the Creation of a Global People's Assembly: Legitimacy and the Power of Popular Sovereignty', *Stanford Journal of International Law* 36/2: 191–219.

Feher, Michel (ed.) (2007). *Nongovernmental Politics*. US: Zone Books.

Ferejohn, J. (1999). 'Accountability and Authority: Toward a Theory of Political Accountability', in *Democracy, Accountability, and Representation*, ed. A. Przeworski, S. Strokes, and B. Manin. Cambridge: Cambridge University Press, pp. 131–53.

Ferguson, Niall (2001). *The Cash Nexus: Money and Power in the Modern World 1700–2000*. London: Allen Lane.

Fishkin, James (1995). *The Voice of the People*. New Haven, Conn.: Yale University Press.

Fixdal, Jon (1997). 'Consensus Conferences as "Extended Peer Groups"', *Science and Public Policy*, 24/6: 366–76.

Forsyth, Murray (1987). *Reason and Revolution. The Political Thought of the Abbé Sieyès*. Leicester: Leicester University Press.

Galtung, J. (2000). 'Alternative Models for Global Democracy', in *Global Democracy: Key Debates*, ed. B. Holden. London: Routledge, pp. 143–61.

Glover, Samuel D. (1999). 'The Putney Debates: Popular versus Elitist Republicanism', *Past and Present* 164/1: 47–80.

Gordon, W. (1994). *The United Nations at the Crossroads of Reform*. New York and London: M. E. Sharpe.

Gould, Carol (1996). 'Diversity and Democracy: Representing Differences', in *Democracy and Difference. Contesting the Boundaries of the Political*, ed. Seyla Benhabib. Princeton, NJ: Princeton University Press, pp. 171–86.

Grant, Ruth W. and Robert O. Keohane (2005). 'Accountability and Abuses of Power in World Politics', *American Political Science Review* 99/1: 29–43.

Gregory I (1887–99). 'Epistola I, 1', in *Registrum Epistolarum*, ed. P. Edward and L. M. Hartmann, 2 vols. Berlin: Weidmann, I, pp. 1–2.

Griffiths, G. (ed.) (1968). *Representative Government in Western Europe in the Sixteenth Century*. Oxford: Clarendon Press.

Grofman, Bernard (1982). 'Should Representatives Be Typical of Their Constituents?', in *Representation and Redistricting Issues*, ed. Bernard Grofman et al. Lexington, MA: D.C. Heath, pp. 97–9.

Guinier, Lani (1994). *The Tyranny of the Majority: Fundamental Fairness in Representative Democracy*. New York: Free Press.

Habermas, Jürgen (1984). *The Theory of Communicative Action*, trans. Thomas MacCarthy, 2 vols., Boston: Beacon Press.

Habermas, Jürgen (1996). *Between Facts and Norms: Contributions to a Discourse Theory of Law and Democracy*, trans. William Rehg. Cambridge, Mass.: MIT Press.

Habermas, Jürgen (2001). *The Postnational Constellation: Political Essays by Jürgen Habermas*, trans. Max Pensky. Cambridge, UK: Polity.

Hansen, Mogens Herman (1991). *The Athenian Democracy in the Age of Demosthenes*. Cambridge, Mass.: Blackwell.

Hawkins, Darren G., Lake, David A., Nielson, Daniel L. and Tierney, Michael J. (eds) (2006). *Delegation and Agency in International Organisations*. Cambridge, Cambridge University Press.

Hayward, J. (ed.) (1995). *The Crisis of Representation in Europe*. London: Frank Cass.

Held, David (1995). *Democracy and the Global Order*. Cambridge, UK: Polity.

Held, David (1998). 'Democracy and Globalization', in *Reimagining Political Community: Studies in Cosmopolitan Democracy*, ed. D Archibugi, D. Held and M. Kohler. Stanford, Calif.: Stanford University Press, pp. 11–27.

Hertz, Noreena (2004). *IOU: The Debt Threat and Why We Must Defuse It*. London: Fourth Estate.

Hirst, Derek (1975). *The Representative of the People? Voters and Voting in England under the Early Stuarts*. Cambridge: Cambridge University Press.

Hobbes, Thomas ([1651] 1996), *Leviathan, or The Matter, Forme, & Power of a Common-Wealth Ecclesiasticall and Civill*, ed. Richard Tuck. Cambridge: Cambridge University Press.

Hofmann, H. (1974). *Repräsentation. Studien zur Wort- und Begriffsgeschichte von der Antike bis ins 19. Jahrhundert*. Berlin: Duncker & Humblot.

Hood, Christopher and Heald, David (eds) (2006). *Transparency: The Key to Better Governance*. Oxford: Oxford University Press.

Htun, Mala (2004). 'Is Gender like Ethnicity? The Political Representation of Identity Groups', *Perspectives on Politics* 2/3: 439–58.

Institutes of Justinian, The (1906), trans. J. B. Moyle, Oxford: Clarendon Press.

Jackson, John E. and King, David C. (1989). 'Public Goods, Private Interests, and Representation', *American Political Science Review* 83/4: 1143–64.

Jaume, Lucien (1986). *Hobbes et l'État représentatif moderne*. Paris: Presses Universitaires de France.

Kateb, George (1992). 'The Moral Distinctiveness of Representative Democracy', in *The Inner Ocean*. Ithaca, NY: Cornell University Press, pp. 36–56.

Kavka, Gregory and Warren, Virginia (1983). 'Political Representation for Future Generations', in *Environmental Philosophy*, ed. R. Elliot and A. Gare. University Park: The Pennsylvania State University Press, pp. 21–39.

Kelly, D. (2004). 'Carl Schmitt's Political Theory of Representation', *Journal of the History of Ideas* 65/1: 113–34.

Koenigsberger, H. G. (1961). 'The Powers of Deputies in Sixteenth-Century Assemblies', in *Album Helen Maud Cam*, II, Louvain, pp. 211–43.

Kornhauser, L. A. and Sager, L. G. (1993). 'The One and the Many: Adjudication in Collegial Courts', *California Law Review* 81: 1–59.

Kuper, Andrew (2004). *Democracy beyond Borders. Justice and Representation in Global Institutions.* Oxford: Oxford University Press.

Kymlicka, Will (1995). *Multicultural Citizenship: A Liberal Theory of Minority Rights.* Oxford: Oxford University Press.

Lefort, Claude (1988). *Democracy and Political Theory.* Minneapolis: University of Minnesota Press.

Locke, John ([1689] 1988). *Two Treatises of Government*, ed. Peter Laslett. Cambridge: Cambridge University Press.

Lublin, David (1997). *The Paradox of Representation: Racial Gerrymandering and Minority Interests in Congress.* Princeton: Princeton University Press.

Madison, James, Hamilton, Alexander and Jay, John ([1787–88] 2005). *The Federalist*, ed. J. R. Pole. Indianapolis: Hackett Publishing Company.

Maitland, F. W. (2003). *State, Trust and Corporation*, ed. David Runciman and Magnus Ryan. Cambridge: Cambridge University Press.

Majone, Giandomenico (2001). 'Two Logics of Delegation: Agency and Fiduciary Relations in EU Governance', *European Union Politics* 2/1: 103–22.

Manin, Bernard (1997). *Modern Representative Government.* Cambridge: Cambridge University Press.

Manin, Bernard, Prezworski, Adam and Strokes, Susan (1999). *Democracy, Accountability, and Representation.* Cambridge: Cambridge University Press.

Mansbridge, Jane (1981). 'Living with Conflict: Representation in the Theory of Adversary Democracy', *Ethics* 91/1: 466–76.

Mansbridge, Jane (1999). 'Should Blacks Represent Blacks and Women Represent Women? A Contingent "Yes"', *Journal of Politics* 61/3: 628–57.

Mansbridge, Jane (2003). 'Rethinking Representation', *American Political Science Review* 97/4: 515–28.

Marsilius of Padua ([1324] 2005). *The Defender of the Peace* (*Defensor pacis*), ed. and trans. Annabel Brett. Cambridge: Cambridge University Press.

Mendle, Michael (ed.) (2001). *The Putney Debates of 1647: The Army, the Levellers and the English State*, Cambridge: Cambridge University Press.

Michels, Robert (1999). *Political Parties: A Sociological Study of the Oligarchical Tendencies of Modern Democracy*, int. Seymour Martin Lipset. New Brunswick, NJ: Transaction Publishers.

Mill, James (1992). *Political Writings*, ed. Terence Ball. Cambridge: Cambridge University Press.

Mill, John Stuart ([1861] 1991). 'Considerations on Representative Government', in *On Liberty and Other Essays*. Oxford: Oxford University Press, pp. 203–467.

Monbiot, George (2003). *The Age of Consent*. London: Flamingo.

Monbiot, George (2006). *Manifesto for a New World Order*. New York, NY: The New Press.

Mosca, Gaetano (1939). *The Ruling Class*, ed. Arthur Livingston. London: McGraw-Hill.

Muller, A. S., Raic, D. and Thuranszky, J. (eds) (1997). *The International Court of Justice: Its Future Role After Fifty Years*. The Hague: Martinus Nijhoff.

Muller, J. (ed.) (1997). *Reforming the United Nations: New Initiatives and Past Efforts*. The Hague: Kluwer Law International.

Näsström, Sofia (2006). 'Representative Democracy as Tautology: Ankersmit and Lefort on Representation', *European Journal of Political Theory* 5/3: 321–42.

Neale, J. E. (1953). *Elizabeth I and Her Parliaments, 1559–1581*, 2 vols. London: Cape.

O'Neill, Brendan (2005). 'What Do Pop Stars Know about the World?', *BBC News Magazine*, 28 June: <www.news.bbc.co.uk/magazine/4629851.stm>.

O'Neill, John (2001). 'Representing People, Representing Nature, Representing the World', *Environment and Planning C: Government and Policy* 19: 483–500.

O'Neill, Onora (2002). *A Question of Trust*. Cambridge: Cambridge University Press.

Ostrogorski, Moisei (1964). *Democracy and the Organisation of Political Parties*, ed. Seymour Martin Lipset. Chicago: Quadrangle.

[Overton, Richard] (1647). *An Appeale From the degenerate Representative Body*. London.

Paine, Thomas (1989), *Political Writings*, ed. Bruce Kuklick. Cambridge: Cambridge University Press.

Paravicini-Bagliani (2000). *The Pope's Body*, trans. David S. Peterson. Chicago, Ill.: University of Chicago Press.

Pareto, Vilfredo (1997). 'The Governing Elite in Present-Day Democracy', in *Classes and Elites in Democracy and Democratization*. New York: Garland, pp. 47–52.

[Parker, Henry] (1642a). *Some Few Observations*. London.

[Parker, Henry] (1642b). *Observations upon His Majesties Late Answers and Expresses*, London.

[Parker, Henry] (1644). *Jus populi: Or, A discourse wherein clear satisfaction is given, as well concerning the right of subiects, as the right of princes*. London.

Parkinson, John (2004). 'Hearing Voices: Negotiating Representation Claims in Public Deliberation', *British Journal of Politics and International Relations* 6/3: 370–88.

Pennington, Kenneth (2006). 'Representation in Medieval Canon Law', in *Repraesentatio: Mapping a Keyword for Churches and Governance*, ed. Massimo Faggioli and Alberto Melloni. Berlin: PLIT Verlag, pp. 21–39.

Pettit, Philip (1999). *Republicanism. A Theory of Freedom and Government*. Oxford: Oxford University Press.

Pettit, Philip (2003). 'Groups with Minds of Their Own', in *Socializing Metaphysics*, ed. F. Schmitt. New York: Rowman & Littlefield, pp. 167–94.

Pettit, Philip (2006). 'Concepts of Representation', paper for Yale symposium on *Representation and Popular Rule*.

Pettit, Philip (2007). *Made with Words. Hobbes on Language, Mind and Politics*. Princeton: Princeton University Press.

Pettit, P. and D. Schweikard (2006). 'Joint Action and Group Agency', *Philosophy of the Social Sciences* 36: 18–39.

Phillips, Anne (1960). 'How Can One Person Represent Another?', *Proceedings of the Aristotelian Society*, Supp. 34: 87–208.

Phillips, Anne (1995). *The Politics of Presence*. Oxford: Clarendon Press.

Phillips, Anne (1998). 'Democracy and Representation: Or, Why Should it Matter Who Our Representatives Are?', in *Feminism and Politics*. Oxford: Oxford University Press, pp. 224–40.

Pitkin, Hanna (1967). *The Concept of Representation*. Berkeley: University of California Press.

Pitkin, Hanna (1968). 'Commentary: The Paradox of Representation', *Nomos* (X [*Representation*]), pp. 38–42.

Pitkin, Hanna (ed.) (1969). *Representation*. New York: Atherton Press.

Pitkin, Hanna (1989). 'Representation', in *Political Innovation and Conceptual Change*. Cambridge: Cambridge University Press, pp. 132–54.

Pliny, the Elder (1952). *Natural History*, trans. H. Rackham, 10 vols. Cambridge, Mass., and London: Harvard University Press, IX.

Plotke, David (1997). 'Representation is Democracy', *Constellations* 4/1: 19–34.

Podlech, Adalbert (1972–97). 'Repräsentation', in *Geschichtliche Grundbegriffe: Historisches Lexikon zur politisch-sozialen Sprache in Deutschland*, ed. Reinhart Koselleck et al., 8 vols. Stuttgart: E. Klett, V, pp. 509–47.

Posner, Eric A. and Figueiredo, Miguel de (2004). 'Is the International Court of Justice Biased?', *University of Chicago Law and Economics Paper* 234.

Post, Gaines (1943). 'Roman Law and Early Representation in Spain and Italy, 1150–1250, *Speculum* 18: 211–32.

Post, Gaines (1964). *Studies in Medieval Legal Thought: Public Law and the State, 1100–1322*. Princeton, NJ: Princeton University Press.

Preston, Michael (1978). 'Black Elected Officials and Public Policy: Symbolic and Substantive Representation', *Political Studies* 7/2: 196–201.

Przeworski, Adam (1999). 'Minimalist Conceptions of Democracy', in *Democracy's Value*, ed. Ian Shapiro and Casiano Hacker-Cordon. Cambridge: Cambridge University Press, pp. 23–55.

Przeworski, Adam, Stokes, Susan and Manin, Bernard (eds) (1999). *Democracy, Accountability and Representation*. Cambridge: Cambridge University Press.

Quillet, J. (1988). 'Community, Counsel and Representation', in *The Cambridge History of Medieval Political Thought, c.350–c.1450*, ed. J. H. Burns. Cambridge: Cambridge University Press, pp. 520–72.

Quintilian (2001). The Orator's Education (*Institutio Oratoria*), ed. and trans. D. A. Russell, 5 vols. Cambridge, Mass., and London: Harvard University Press, III.

Rausch, Heinz Volker (1968). *Zur Theorie und Geschichte der Repräsentation und Repräsentativverfassung*. Darmstadt: Wissenschaftliche Buchgesellschaft.

Rawls, John (1993). *Political Liberalism*. New York: Columbia University Press.

Rawls, John (1999). *A Theory of Justice*, rev. edn. Cambridge Mass.: Harvard University Press.

Rees, Martin (2003). *Our Final Century? Will the Human Race Survive the Twenty-first Century?* London: William Heinemann.

Rehfeld, Andrew (2005). *The Concept of Constituency. Political Representation, Democratic Legitimacy, and Institutional Design*. Cambridge: Cambridge University Press.

Rehfeld, Andrew (2006). 'Towards a General Theory of Political Representation', *Journal of Politics* 68/1: 1–21.

Rogowski, R. (1981). 'Representation in Political Theory and Law', *Ethics* 91/3: 395–430.

Romano, C. P. R. (1999). 'The Proliferation of International Judicial Bodies: The Pieces of the Puzzle', *New York University Journal of International Law and Politics* 31: 709–51.

Rosanvallon, Pierre (1998). *Le people introuvable. Histoire de la représentation democratique en France*. Paris: Gallimard.

Rosanvallon, Pierre (2006). *La contre-démocratie*. Paris: Seuil.

Rousseau, Jean-Jacques (1997). *The Social Contract and Other Later Political Writings*, ed. Victor Gourevitch. Cambridge: Cambridge University Press.

Rousseau, Jean-Jacques (2004). *Letter to D'Alembert and Writings for the Theater*, ed. Allan Bloom et al., in *The Collected Writings of Rousseau*, 11 vols. Hanover and London: University Press of New England, X.

Runciman, David (1997). *Pluralism and the Personality of the State*. Cambridge: Cambridge University Press.

Runciman, David (2003). 'Moral Responsibility and the Problem of Representing the State', in *Can Institutions Have Responsibilities? Collective Moral Agency and International Relations*, ed. Toni Erskine. Basingstoke: Palgrave Macmillan, pp. 41–51.

Runciman, David (2007). 'The Paradox of Political Representation', *Journal of Political Philosophy* 15/1: 93–114.

Russell, Conrad (1983). 'The Nature of a Parliament in Early Stuart England', in *Before the Civil War. Essay on Early Stuart Politics and Government*, ed. Howard Tomlinson. London, Macmillan, pp. 123–50.

Ryden, David K (1996). *Representation in Crisis*. New York: State University of New York Press.

Sanderson, John (1989). *'But the People's Creatures': The Philosophical Basis of the English Civil War*. Manchester: Manchester University Press.

Sapiro, Virginia (1981). 'When are Interests Interesting? The Problem of Political Representation of Women', *American Political Science Review* 75/3: 701–16.

Schmitt, Carl (1985). *Political Theology*, trans. George Schwab. Cambridge, Mass.: MIT Press.

Schmitt, Carl (1988). *The Crisis of Parliamentary Democracy*, trans. Ellen Kennedy. Cambridge, Mass.: MIT Press.

Schmitt, Carl (1996a). *Roman Catholicism and Political Form*, trans. G. L. Ulmen. Westport, Conn.: Greenwood Press.

Schmitt, Carl (1996b). *The Concept of the Political*, trans. George Schwab. Chicago: Chicago University Press.

Schumpeter, J. A. ([1942] 1976). *Capitalism, Socialism and Democracy*, ed. R. Swedberg. London: Routledge.

Seaward, Paul (2006). 'Representation and Parliament', in *Repraesentatio: Mapping a Keyword for Churches and Governance*, ed. Massimo Faggioli and Alberto Melloni. Berlin: PLIT Verlag, pp. 125–49.

Seitz, Brian (1995). *The Trace of Political Representation*. Albany, NY: State University of New York Press.

Shapiro, Ian (2003). *The State of Democratic Theory*. Princeton: Princeton University Press.

Siedentop, Larry (2001). *Democracy in Europe*. New York: Columbia University Press.

Sieyès, Emmanuel Joseph (1795). *Opinion de Sieyès, sur plusieurs articles des titres IV et V du projet de constitution, prononcé à la Convention le 9 thermidor de l'an troisième de la République*. Paris: Imprimerie nationale.

Sieyès, Emmanuel Joseph (1985). *Écrits politiques*, ed. Roberto Zapperi. Paris: Éditions des Archives Contemporaines.

Sieyès, Emmanuel Joseph (2003). *Political Writings*, ed. Michael Sonenscher. Indianapolis: Hackett Publishing Company.

Skinner, Quentin (2005). 'Hobbes on Representation', *European Journal of Philosophy* 13/2: 155–84.

Slaughter, A.-M. (2004). *A New World Order*. Princeton, NJ: Princeton University Press.

Smith, Sir Thomas ([1581] 1982), *De republica anglorum*, ed. Mary Dewar. Cambridge: Cambridge University Press.

Steinberg, Richard H. (2004). 'Judicial Lawmaking at the WTO: Discursive Constitutional and Political Constraints', *American Journal of International Law* 98/2: 247–75.

Stimson, James A., Mackuen, Michael B. and Erikson, Robert S. (1995). 'Dynamic Representation', *American Political Science Review* 89/3: 543–65.

Stoker, G. (2006). *Why Politics Matters: Making Democracy Work* (Basingstoke: Palgrave).

Strong, Tracy and Dugan, C. N. (2001). 'Music, Politics, Theatre and Representation in Rousseau', in *The Cambridge Companion to Rousseau*, ed. Patrick Riley. Cambridge: Cambridge University Press, pp. 329–64.

Swain, Carol M. (1993). *Black Faces, Black Interests: The Representation of African Americans in Congress*. Cambridge, Mass.: Harvard University Press.

Taylor, Charles (1994). *Multiculturalism: Examining the Politics of Recognition*. Princeton: Princeton University Press.

Thakur, R. (ed.) (1998). *Past Imperfect, Future Uncertain: The United Nations at Fifty*. Basingstoke: Macmillan.

Thomas, Sue (1991). 'The Impact of Women on State Legislative Policies', *Journal of Politics* 53/4: 958–76.

Thompson, Dennis (2005). 'Democracy in Time: Popular Sovereignty and Temporal Representation', *Constellations* 12/2: 245–61.

Tierney, Brian (1982). *Religion, Law, and the Growth of Constitutional Thought, 1150–1650*. Cambridge: Cambridge University Press.

Tierney, Brian (1983). 'The Idea of Representation in the Medieval Councils of the West', *Concilium* 19: 25–30.

Tocqueville, Alexis de ([1835–1840] 2002). *Democracy in America*, ed. Harvey C. Mansfield. Chicago, Ill., and London: University of Chicago Press.

UN (1995). United Nations Open-ended Working Group on the Question of Equitable Representation on and Increase in the Membership of the Security Council and Other Matters Related to the Security Council, 'Annex to the Report [of 15 September 1995]', New York: United Nations.

Urbinati, Nadia (2000). 'Representation as Advocacy: A Study of Democratic Deliberation', *Political Theory* 28/6: 758–86.

Urbinati, Nadia (2006). *Representative Democracy: Principles and Genealogy*. Chicago, Ill., and London: University of Chicago Press.

Van Parijs, Phillipe (1998). 'The Disenfranchisement of the Elderly and Other Attempts to Secure Intergenerational Justice', *Philosophy and Public Affairs* 27/4: 292–333.

Weber, Max (1994). *Political Writings*, ed. Peter Lassman and Ronald Speirs. Cambridge: Cambridge University Press.

Wendt, A. (2003). 'Why a World State is Inevitable', *European Journal of International Relations* 9/4: 491–542.

Weissberg, Robert (1978). 'Collective vs. Dyadic Representation in Congress', *American Political Science Review* 72/2: 535–47.

Wilks, M. (1972). 'Corporation and Representation in the *Defensor Pacis*', *Studia Gratiana* 15: 253–92.

Williams, Melissa (1998). *Voice, Trust, and Memory: Marginalized Groups and the Failings of Liberal Representation*. Princeton, NJ: Princeton University Press.

Wood, Gordon S. (1998). *The Creation of the American Republic, 1776–1787*. North Carolina: University of North Carolina Press.

Wood, Gordon S. (2003). *The American Revolution: A History*. London: Weidenfeld & Nicolson.

Woods, Ngaire (2000). 'The Challenges of Multilateralism and Governance', in *The World Bank: Policies and Structure*, ed.

Chris Gilbert and David Vines. Cambridge: Cambridge University Press, pp. 132–56.

Woods, Ngaire (2006). *The Globalizers: The FMI, the World Bank, and Their Borrowers*. Ithaca, NY, and London: Cornell University Press.

Wootton, David (1991). 'Leveller Democracy and the Puritan Revolution', in *The Cambridge History of Political Thought, 1450–1700*, ed. J. H. Burns. Cambridge: Cambridge University Press, pp. 412–42.

Young, Iris Marion (1990). *Justice and the Politics of Difference*. Princeton, NJ: Princeton University Press.

Young, Iris Marion (1997). 'Deferring Group Representation', in *Nomos XXXIX: Ethnicity and Group Rights*, ed. Ian Shapiro and Will Kymlicka. New York: New York University Press, pp. 349–76.

Young, Iris Marion (2000). *Inclusion and Democracy*. Oxford: Oxford University Press.

Zaret, D. (2000). *Origins of Democratic Culture: Printing, Petitions and the Public Sphere in Early Modern England*. Princeton: Princeton University Press.

Index